CW01509532

Christmas Voices

Reflections, carols, poems &
prayers for the festive season

Reflections by Claire Musters

with Naomi Aidoo, Andy Angel, Jonathan Arnold, Imogen Ball, Ruth M. Bancewicz, Carl Beech, John L. Bell, Andrew Boakye, Catherine Butcher, Lyndall Bywater, Mags Duggan, Hannah Fytche, Gordon Giles, Paul W. Goodliff, Isabelle Hamley, Clare Hayns, Liz Hoare, Trystan Owain Hughes, Lakshmi Jeffreys, Andy Kind, David Kitchen, Esther Kuku, Martin Leckebusch, Bekah Legg, Ann Lewin, Tanya Marlow, Leoné Martin, Chine McDonald, Lucy Moore, Michele D. Morrison, Charmaine Noble-McLean, Emma Pennington, Pam Rhodes, Amy Scott Robinson, Margaret Silf, Meric Srokosz, Jo Swinney, Rachele Vernon O'Brien, Sally Welch and Natalie Williams

BRF

15 The Chambers, Vineyard
Abingdon OX14 3FE
brf.org.uk

Bible Reading Fellowship (BRF) is a charity (233280)
and company limited by guarantee (301324),
registered in England and Wales

ISBN 978 1 80039 230 4
First published 2023
10 9 8 7 6 5 4 3 2 1 0
All rights reserved

Acknowledgements

Unless otherwise stated, scripture quotations marked NIV are taken from The Holy Bible, New International Version®, NIV® Copyright © 1973, 1978, 1984, 2011 by Biblica, Inc.® Used by permission. All rights reserved worldwide.

'Prayer of blessing (Christmas)' from *Common Worship: Services and Prayers for the Church of England* is © The Archbishops' Council 2005. Published by Church House Publishing. Used by permission. **rights@hymnsam.co.uk**

'Bethlehem Down' by Peter Warlock and Bruce Blunt © Copyright 1928 by Hawkes & Son (London) Ltd. Reproduced by permission of Boosey & Hawkes Music Publishers Ltd.

A catalogue record for this book is available from the British Library

Printed and bound by Ashford Colour Press

Contents

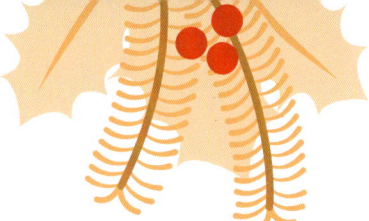

Love 127

O holy night

Introduction

Whether you're picking up this book at the beginning of Advent or reading it over Christmas itself, *Christmas Voices* offers a series of precious moments to reflect and rest in God's presence.

The five sections of the book explore God's promises, the theme of preparation and making ready, and then a powerful trio of gifts: joy, peace and love. Each day, a Bible passage is followed by a reflection. We then include a hymn, carol, poem or prayer* selected by one of our 'choir of voices', who have each chosen a favourite piece and shared with us why it is special to them.

It has been fascinating to see what everyone sent in; if it had been a competition, 'O holy night' would have undoubtedly taken first prize; no fewer than seven people chose it. We therefore place this wonderful song at the start of the book and return to it as an introduction to our closing section on 'Love'.

We hope that all of these different voices, experiences and perspectives weave a satisfyingly rich tapestry, and that this book will be one you dip into time and again.

* Please note that some of the longer hymns and carols have been abbreviated.

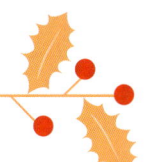

The promise

O holy night

O holy night, the stars are brightly shining;
It is the night of the dear Saviour's birth.
Long lay the world in sin and error pining,
Till he appeared and the soul felt its worth.
A thrill of hope – the weary world rejoices,
For yonder breaks a new and glorious morn!

Fall on your knees, Oh hear the angel voices!
O night divine, O night when Christ was born!
O night, O holy night, O night divine.

Led by the light of faith serenely beaming,
With glowing hearts by his cradle we stand.
So, led by light of a star sweetly gleaming,
Here come the wise men from Orient land.
The king of kings lay thus in lowly manger,
In all our trials born to be our friend.

He knows our need – to our weakness is no stranger.
Behold your king, before him lowly bend!
Behold your king, before him lowly bend!

Truly He taught us to love one another;
His law is Love and his gospel is peace.
Chains shall he break, for the slave is our brother,
And in his name all oppression shall cease.
Sweet hymns of joy in grateful chorus raise we;
Let all within us praise his holy name.

Christ is the Lord! O praise his name forever!
His pow'r and glory evermore proclaim!
His pow'r and glory evermore proclaim!

Words by Placide Cappeau (1808–77), translated by John Sullivan Dwight (1813–93); music by Adolphe Adam (1803–56)

The lines 'Chains shall he break, for the slave is our brother, And in his name all oppression shall cease' never fail to give me goosebumps. In these lines, I see the Jesus I love: one that calls us to love each other – no matter our background – and invites us to break all oppression and injustice alongside him.

Chine McDonald, director, Theos

My favourite carol is 'O holy night'. Its beautiful melody leaves me wanting to close my eyes and just lose myself in the voices, but the lyrics are even more powerful. From the 'thrill of hope' that captures the true joy of Christmas, to the reminder of this king of kings who humbled himself to a lowly manger, to the promise that this baby, this Jesus, will one day break every chain and end all oppression. It's the gospel in three verses and I love it.

Bekah Legg, CEO, Restored

I first heard this beautiful carol many years ago when it was sung by an American high school choir in the city of Taichung, Taiwan. I was a newly arrived missionary, far from home and loved ones, and struggling to find my place in the predominantly American team I had joined. The line 'He knows our need – to our weakness is no stranger' brought me to tears as I realised in a fresh way that Jesus knew exactly what I was going through; knew intimately the weight of homesickness, of not belonging, of feeling different – because he'd been there. He was – and is – no stranger to my weakness, and because of that, he is the safest place of all to bring my needs, my brokenness, my hurts and my hopes. Always.

Mags Duggan, author, spiritual director and retreat leader

Day 1

God the promise keeper

For to us a child is born,
    to us a son is given,
  and the government will be on his shoulders.
And he will be called
    Wonderful Counsellor, Mighty God,
    Everlasting Father, Prince of Peace.
Of the greatness of his government and peace
    there will be no end.
He will reign on David's throne
    and over his kingdom,
establishing and upholding it
    with justice and righteousness
    from that time on and forever.
The zeal of the Lord Almighty
    will accomplish this.

ISAIAH 9:6–7

Reflection

I still find it incredible that God spoke through Old Testament prophets such as Isaiah to let his people throughout the ages know that he had a plan that would rescue us and make all things right. In our reflections, we will look at what he said to both Old and New Testament characters, and their responses, as well as hear from Jesus and the apostles.

Christmas reminds us that God keeps his promises. His plan may not have been what we would have chosen – sending Jesus as a helpless baby. And yet this passage in Isaiah, so often read at Christmas carol services, quickly reveals the significance of this baby boy. He was to bring forth a new government, one of peace (which we will look at later), wonder and might, which will last forever and be accompanied by justice and righteousness. Of course, this came through a 'might' that people were not expecting – the ultimate sacrifice – and we are still to see the complete fulfilment of this prophecy. But it gives us a hope to cling to; that he can take the broken parts of our lives and hold us in them – and still bring about his goodness. Even in those moments when the darkness seems to be overtaking the world (or us as individuals), we can choose to remember the promise that he *is* reigning and he *will* have the last word.

We can be so full of activity in the run-up to the Christmas period – but for all the hours of preparation it is over so quickly. While many of us may enjoy gatherings around glorious feasts, I am aware that for others Christmas brings the sting of loneliness into ever sharper focus. This passage reminds us that we have a promise of something – someone – far greater than even this season; someone who is everlasting, and full of zeal for us and for his promises to us.

Prayer

I thank you, Jesus, for the vulnerability and humility you showed when you came to earth as a baby – and I believe you will fulfil all that this prophecy says. Amen.

Once in royal David's city

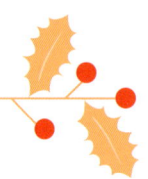

Once in royal David's city
stood a lowly cattle shed,
where a mother laid her baby
in a manger for his bed:
Mary was that mother mild,
Jesus Christ her little child.

He came down to earth from heaven,
who is God and Lord of all,
and his shelter was a stable,
and his cradle was a stall;
with the poor and meek and lowly,
lived on earth our Saviour holy.

Words by Cecil Frances Alexander (1818–95); music by Henry Gauntlett (1805–76)

As a biologist, I am acutely aware that before he was a tiny newborn baby, Jesus was an even tinier embryo: something so fragile that it had to be sheltered in a girl's womb. For me, these verses capture a little of the mind-blowing reality of God becoming so vulnerable that he had to trust himself to human care.

Ruth M. Bancewicz, church engagement director, The Faraday Institute for Science and Religion, Cambridge

I never went to a carol service as a young boy, although I must have sung 'Away in a manger' along with other bits and bobs in primary school. Then I turned eleven and was sent to a terrifyingly large place called secondary school. Mine turned out to be quite posh and held a Christmas service in St Martin-in-the-Fields, just off Trafalgar Square in London. We were expected to find our own way there.

I arrived, got my name ticked off a list, shuffled into the building's vast 18th-century darkness, sat down and waited. Exactly on the hour, I saw a single large candle moving in one corner and a voice rang out with 'Once in royal David's city'.

To me, that was Darian: the thin lad in the year above mine. To others, he was Darian Angadi: the best treble voice of his generation, the boy who sang for Benjamin Britten. It was heart-stopping. I'd thought the Christmas story was a thing for adults which got softened up for us with a bag of presents. That day changed my mind. If it involved a sound so amazing, I had to know more.

David Kitchen, author, poet, broadcaster and teacher

Day 2

Stretched by a promise

The Lord had said to Abram, 'Go from your country, your people and your father's household to the land I will show you.

'I will make you into a great nation,
    and I will bless you;
I will make your name great,
    and you will be a blessing.
I will bless those who bless you,
    and whoever curses you I will curse;
and all peoples on earth
    will be blessed through you.'

So Abram went, as the Lord had told him; and Lot went with him. Abram was seventy-five years old when he set out from Harran.

GENESIS 12:1–4

Reflection

God loves to speak to his people – and to give them promises. Noah, for example, was shown a rainbow as God promised never to send a flood again; Moses was given the promise that God would free his people from slavery in Egypt.

Often God's promises make us uncomfortable, or necessitate action from us. Here, Abram was given an incredible promise – that he would become a great nation and that God would be behind him all the way – but he had to leave all he had known in order for that promise to take place. His faithfulness and hope in that promise was tested to the limit (and he made huge mistakes along the way), but God *always* provided – just perhaps not in the timeline Abram and those in his household wanted!

Have you ever experienced that? A promise from God that you have had to cling on to and perhaps step out into in a way that is uncomfortable or slightly scary? The idea of the promises of God seems so appealing, but often the fulfilment of them stretches us in ways we couldn't have imagined beforehand.

Too often the promise of our coming Saviour is sanitised too – into a beautiful nativity scene. I am sure the reality was very different for his parents – tired and dirty, confused and disappointed that there was no room for them anywhere. Jesus was born into messy circumstances – physically, but also politically and spiritually.

What reassures me is that God loves to involve us in the outworking of his promises, and he doesn't disown us when we fail. It is incredible to think that Abram did indeed become Abraham and that through his line Jesus the Messiah came. But day to day, Abram wouldn't have seen the fulfilment of all that God had said to him, although he did receive the promised son and heir he longed for. He is mentioned in the 'faith hall of fame' in Hebrews 11, where it also says: 'They did not receive the things promised; they only saw them and welcomed them from a distance… They were longing for a better country – a heavenly one' (Hebrews 11:13, 16).

Let us not settle this Christmas season, but press on even when we feel uncomfortable.

Prayer

Lord, I thank you that you give us promises; help me not to shrink when you are urging me to action or stretching me. Amen.

Hail! smiling morn

Hail! smiling morn, smiling morn,
That tips the hills with gold, that tips the hills with gold,
And whose rosy fingers open wide the gates of heaven, the gates of heaven,
And whose rosy fingers open wide the gates of heaven.

All the green fields that natures doth unfold,
All the green fields that natures doth unfold.
At whose bright presence darkness flies away, flies away, flies away,
Darkness flies away, darkness flies away,
At whose bright presence darkness flies away, flies away, flies away,
Darkness flies away, darkness flies away,
Hail! Hail! Hail! Hail!
Hail! Hail! Hail! Hail!

Reginald Spofforth (1769–1827)

We moved house to the Peak District during lockdown, so our first two Christmases in the new parish were pretty gloomy. Only in 2022 did we experience our first Derbyshire Christmas, with local carols we hadn't had the chance to hear before. Belting out 'Hail! smiling morn' with local carol singers, jammed into the bar of The Scotsman's Pack, the pub below the church, was a bright sign of hope, like the words of the song itself. Having a new Ukrainian baby in the house made Christmas even more poignant. With the new start signalled by the birth of both Jesus and the refugee child of 2022, we could begin to look forward, like standing in the dawn of a new day.

Lucy Moore, founder of Messy Church and head of the Church of England's Growing Faith Foundation

Day 3

Heart response

The angel said to her, 'Do not be afraid, Mary, you have found favour with God. You will conceive and give birth to a son, and you are to call him Jesus. He will be great and will be called the Son of the Most High. The Lord God will give him the throne of his father David, and he will reign over Jacob's descendants forever; his kingdom will never end.'

'How will this be,' Mary asked the angel, 'since I am a virgin?'

The angel answered, 'The Holy Spirit will come on you, and the power of the Most High will overshadow you. So the holy one to be born will be called the Son of God. Even Elizabeth your relative is going to have a child in her old age, and she who was said to be unable to conceive is in her sixth month. For no word from God will ever fail.'

'I am the Lord's servant,' Mary answered. 'May your word to me be fulfilled.' Then the angel left her.

LUKE 1:30–38

Reflection

This is a famous passage. And yet do we take time to really consider how incredible – and disturbing – the encounter actually was? Just ponder: an angel visited a young girl who was told she was about to become pregnant without ever having sex!

I think I would have had far more questions than Mary, although we are told in an earlier verse that she was 'greatly troubled' (v. 29). There was probably a whole rush of emotions and thoughts invading her body and mind throughout their conversation, but the angel provided reassurance that God had seen her, knew her and had chosen her. This must have caused a heart response, given the humility of her final words: 'I am the Lord's servant… May your word to me be fulfilled' (v. 38).

This was a promise that would cause huge upheaval for Mary, had the potential to ruin her reputation – and would take place inside her body! And yet she accepted the angel's words, and submitted to the promise.

Often we can start the Advent period with good intentions about slowing down and focusing on the real meaning of the season, and then get bombarded with thoughts about what presents to buy, decorating our homes and catering for large numbers. Or perhaps we become overwhelmed by feelings of loneliness and pain as Christmas draws ever closer and we are reminded of how alone we are.

Whatever our situation, it is so helpful to pause for a moment and ask: where is my heart? So let me ask you: what is it that you are focusing your attention on right now? Are you fearful? Do you need to hear again the message that God sees and knows you? Mary's heart response can encourage us all to humble ourselves, however rushed or quiet our days are.

I am also struck afresh by the means by which God chose to send Jesus to earth. It is a reminder that we do not need to seek after perfection – it was to a lowly position of utter vulnerability that he came. He grew in the secret place of Mary's womb; how is God inviting you to grow in the secret place of his presence today?

Prayer

Lord, thank you that you see me. Help me to submit myself fully to you today.

There is no rose of such virtue

There is no rose of such virtue
As is the rose that bare Jesu;
Alleluia.

For in this rose contained was
Heaven and earth in little space;
Res miranda.

By that rose we may well see
That he is God in persons three,
Pari forma.

The angels sungen the shepherds to:
Gloria in excelsis Deo:
Gaudeamus.

Leave we all this worldly mirth,
And follow we this joyful birth;
Transeamus.

Anonymous, 15th century;
composers include
Benjamin Britten (1913–76)

One of the earliest surviving English texts for a carol is 'Ther is no rose of swych virtu', and I love it for the phrase 'heaven and earth in little space'. It is an extraordinary biblical truth to hold together the cosmic Christ, the one who 'flung stars into space', in the vivid phrase of Graham Kendrick's song 'The Servant King', and the baby growing in Mary's womb with his tiny hands ready to grip Mary's finger with the reflex grasp of the newborn.

'Heaven and earth in little space', the creator growing in his creature's body; the eternal logos, the Word of God, restricted to a simple cry as his only means of communication; and the bread of life at his mother's breast and laid in a stable's feeding trough.

Paul W. Goodliff, associate research fellow, Spurgeon's College, and convenor, The Order for Baptist Ministry

Day 4

A costly calling

Mary was pledged to be married to Joseph, but before they came together, she was found to be pregnant through the Holy Spirit. Because Joseph her husband was faithful to the law, and yet did not want to expose her to public disgrace, he had in mind to divorce her quietly.

But after he had considered this, an angel of the Lord appeared to him in a dream and said, 'Joseph son of David, do not be afraid to take Mary home as your wife, because what is conceived in her is from the Holy Spirit. She will give birth to a son, and you are to give him the name Jesus, because he will save his people from their sins.'

MATTHEW 1:18–21

Reflection

Here we look at the promise of Jesus' birth again, but from the perspective of what it meant for Joseph. We are told that he was an upstanding member of society and looked for a way to remove himself from the delicate situation without publicly humiliating Mary. And yet as soon as he had those thoughts, he, too, was visited by an angel, who reiterated the promise.

But what did this conversation mean for Joseph? The road ahead for him was probably incredibly lonely at times. He may have had moments in which he wrestled with insecurity, as he watched Mary blossom and then give birth to Jesus – knowing the incredible future this baby had, and yet he wasn't his. Those around them may have misunderstood and questioned his decision to stay with Mary or made assumptions about their relationship, but he was resolutely obedient in the face of the promise. Incredibly, he too was included in the details; Jesus' name was revealed to him too. What a privilege that was – but what a costly calling.

Have there been times when you have felt misunderstood? Overlooked? Know that God sees and appreciates your obedience and knows when it is costly. Joseph had a vital part in caring for the mother of Jesus, and for Jesus himself as he grew from baby to child and possibly to adult (there is no mention of him once Jesus started his public ministry).

You, too, have a vital role in God's plans, whether that is seen by many or hidden. I remember my mum struggling as her health deteriorated, upset that she couldn't 'do' much for God anymore. But he showed her how much he valued the hours of prayer she undertook while she sat on her sofa daily.

Joseph would have taken care to teach Jesus, all the while knowing that he would need to let go, as he had been told from the start what Jesus' mission was. God often asks us to hold even those things he has called us to lightly, which can, again, feel costly. But, while we can rejoice that God loves to include us in his plans, the activities and roles are never to take the place of our Saviour in our hearts.

Prayer

Lord, I recognise that it is both a privilege and costly to follow you. I choose to be mindful of both today.

Coventry Carol

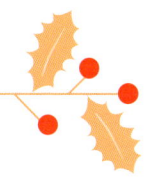

Lully, lullah, thou little tiny child,
bye bye, lully, lullay.
Thou little tiny child,
bye bye, lully, lullay.

O sisters too, how may we do
for to preserve this day
this poor youngling for whom we sing,
'Bye bye, lully, lullay'?

Herod the king, in his raging,
chargèd he hath this day
his men of might, in his own sight,
all young children to slay.

That woe is me, poor child, for thee
and ever mourn and may
for thy parting neither say nor sing,
'Bye bye, lully, lullay.'

Oldest known text by Robert Croo, 16th century;
music attributed to Thomas Mawdyke, 16th century

As a writer whose work explores honest prayer in the midst of suffering, I love the 'Coventry Carol'. Sung in a minor key, imagining the lament of the grieving mothers of the babies slaughtered by Herod, it boldly acknowledges the evils of the world. Christmases in today's world can similarly hold much grief and evil. Yet there is hope, shown musically by the resolution in a major key and by the final chorus, hinting at the vulnerable baby who grew into a 'man of sorrows' – Jesus, the Saviour of us all, who knows our suffering.

Tanya Marlow, author of *Those Who Wait*

Day 5

Our living hope

In his great mercy he has given us new birth into a living hope through the resurrection of Jesus Christ from the dead, and into an inheritance that can never perish, spoil or fade. This inheritance is kept in heaven for you, who through faith are shielded by God's power until the coming of the salvation that is ready to be revealed in the last time. In all this you greatly rejoice, though now for a little while you may have had to suffer grief in all kinds of trials.

1 PETER 1:3–6

Reflection

During this season we tend to focus on Jesus' coming to earth, the image of him as a helpless baby. And yet the promise that is held within the Christmas message is salvation – 'living hope' – which only came about after his appalling suffering, death and then glorious resurrection. I find it helpful to hold the full picture in my mind.

While we celebrate Jesus' birth at Christmas, we too have been given a new birth – into that hope and promise of our inheritance, which we partly enjoy now, but will only be fully realised in heaven. Interestingly, this passage indicates that it is our faith that unlocks God's protection, but also that we can rejoice in what is to come, even though we endure difficult times.

We don't tend to look at suffering at Christmas, but it is foolish to try to decorate over the cracks in order to project a shiny image. When we do this – either in our churches or friendship circles – it makes it more difficult for everyone to truly enter into the season. Rather than embracing hope, we can grit our teeth and just try to get on with things. It is far better to be honest about our trials, but also invite Jesus into them.

Later in this passage it talks about our faith being 'of greater worth than gold, which perishes even though refined by fire' (1 Peter 1:7). I wonder what this season would look like, and how our faith would be shaped, if we genuinely sat with the realities of joyful hope and deep suffering, allowing them to be held in tension before Jesus.

The world feels like it is getting darker and life more difficult to navigate, and yet we *do* have a future that will never perish. Jesus can shine his light in us and through us, whatever our circumstances. I love the image of a cracked pot and how light doesn't shine through it apart from at those broken places. We have 'this treasure in jars of clay' (2 Corinthians 4:7): this doesn't negate the treasure within, but rather acknowledges our vulnerability. The wonder of the promise of salvation is that God works in our weakness, and through our suffering.

Prayer

Lord, I thank you for the living hope that I can experience now, even in the midst of suffering.

O come, O come, Emmanuel

O come, O come, Emmanuel,
and ransom captive Israel,
that mourns in lonely exile here,
until the Son of God appear.
Rejoice! Rejoice! Emmanuel
shall come to thee, O Israel.

O come, thou Rod of Jesse, free
thine own from Satan's tyranny;
from depths of hell thy people save,
and give them victory o'er the grave.
Rejoice! Rejoice! Emmanuel
shall come to thee, O Israel.

O come, thou Dayspring, from on high,
and cheer us by thy drawing nigh;
disperse the gloomy clouds of night,
and death's dark shadows put to flight.
Rejoice! Rejoice! Emmanuel
shall come to thee, O Israel.

O come, thou Key of David, come
and open wide our heav'nly home;
make safe the way that leads on high,
and close the path to misery.
Rejoice! Rejoice! Emmanuel
shall come to thee, O Israel.

O come, Adonai, Lord of might,
who to thy tribes, on Sinai's height,
in ancient times didst give the law
in cloud and majesty and awe.
Rejoice! Rejoice! Emmanuel
shall come to thee, O Israel.

Translated by John Mason Neale (1818–66) from Latin original;
music by Thomas Helmore based on anonymous 15th-century melody

I love the carol 'O come, O come, Emmanuel'. There is so much sparkle and false cheer around in the Christmas season, and this carol expresses the deep and quite painful yearning for rescue, comfort and God's presence experienced by so many throughout history.

Jo Swinney, head of communications at A Rocha International, author and speaker

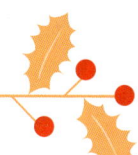

The preparation

In the bleak midwinter

In the bleak midwinter
frosty wind made moan,
earth stood hard as iron,
water like a stone;
snow had fallen,
snow on snow, snow on snow,
in the bleak midwinter
long ago.

Our God, heaven cannot hold him
nor earth sustain;
heaven and earth shall flee away
when he comes to reign:
in the bleak midwinter
a stable place sufficed
the Lord God Almighty,
Jesus Christ.

Angels and archangels
may have gathered there,
cherubim and seraphim
thronged the air;
but only his mother
in her maiden bliss
worshipped the beloved
with a kiss.

What can I give him,
poor as I am?
If I were a shepherd
I would bring a lamb;
If I were a wise man
I would do my part;
yet what I can I give him,
give my heart.

Words by Christina Rossetti (1830–94); music by Gustav Holst (1874–1934),
alternative melody by Harold Darke (1888–1976)

I love this carol, as the last verse sums up what Christmas is really about. The Lord God Almighty giving himself in the person of his Son surely screams for some kind of response. Rossetti asks so brilliantly in her few lines what an appropriate response would look like. I have no idea whether or not Rossetti was a Hebrew scholar, but the heart in Hebrew thought was more than anything else the seat of the volition, our wills. What is Christmas about? Giving God the gift of my will and sacrificing my all for his will.

Andy Angel, director of formation for ministry, Oxford Diocese

Day 6

Delighting in God

Trust in the Lord and do good;
    dwell in the land and enjoy safe pasture.
Take delight in the Lord,
    and he will give you the desires of your heart.
Commit your way to the Lord;
    trust in him and he will do this:
he will make your righteous reward shine like the dawn,
    your vindication like the noonday sun.
Be still before the Lord
    and wait patiently for him;
do not fret when people succeed in their ways,
    when they carry out their wicked schemes.
Refrain from anger and turn from wrath;
    do not fret – it leads only to evil.
For those who are evil will be destroyed,
    but those who hope in the Lord will inherit the land.

PSALM 37:3–9

Reflection

In this psalm we hear David's voice – we will be looking at how he outworked his faith tomorrow. But here he encourages us to 'be still' and 'wait patiently' – two great directives, but, as we've already seen, not so easy to do in our frenetic culture. We are also told not to fret, which seems difficult to do in a world full of wars and other crises. Ultimately, though, God is the one in control, however much it seems that evil is advancing. David also reveals to us a key to being able to wait and trust God: taking delight in him.

When I read the line 'he will give you the desires of your heart' (Psalm 37:4), it reminds me of one of our children, who, come Christmastime, always has a very long wish list. My husband recently explained that a wish list is not something that you should expect to receive everything from, but a list of ideas from which we then have the joy of choosing. Often the expectation and pressure can be that parents should be buying all their children want.

However, when it says here that God will give us our desires, it comes after we have delighted in him. As we get to know him better, our wills become more aligned to his and what we desire reflects his own desires for us.

How do we get to know him better? Regular reading of the Bible, prayer and worship are great starting points – but there are so many other ways, such as through noticing his fingerprints in nature, or savouring a moment's quiet with him. Why not take some time to brainstorm what delighting in God could look like for you?

While being still before God is vital, as it renews us, we are also shown that waiting is active: 'do good; dwell in the land' (v. 3). This reminds me that we are called to be a blessing to our neighbours. As we approach Christmas, people around us may be busy preparing for visits to or from family, or they may be hunkering down knowing they will be alone. How can you take time to reach out to those who live around you this week?

Prayer

Lord, help me to look to you and trust you, take time to delight in you and reach out to those around me with the love you have shown me.

Courage, brother! Do not stumble

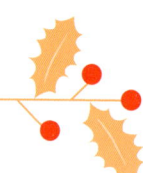

Courage, brother! Do not stumble,
though your path be dark as night;
there's a star to guide the humble:
trust in God, and do the right.
Let the road be rough and dreary,
and its end far out of sight;
foot it bravely; strong or weary,
trust in God, trust in God,
trust in God, and do the right.

Perish policy and cunning,
perish all that fears the light!
Whether losing, whether winning,
trust in God, and do the right.
Some will hate you, some will love you,
some will flatter, some will slight;
heed them not, and look above you:
trust in God, trust in God,
trust in God, and do the right.

Simple rule and safest guiding,
inward peace, and inward might,
star upon our path abiding,
trust in God, and do the right.
Courage, sister! do not stumble,
though your path be dark as night;
there's a star to guide the humble:
trust in God, trust in God,
trust in God, and do the right.

Words by Norman Macleod (1812–72); music 'Courage' by Arthur Sullivan (1842–1900), alternative melody 'Beecher' by John Zundel (1815–82)

This old hymn has always encouraged and reminded me to keep on the narrow path that God has put me on despite any opposition, trial, challenge or disaster. We just have to keep following the light of Christ. As Philippians 3:13–14 says: 'Brothers and sisters, I do not consider myself yet to have taken hold of it. But one thing I do: forgetting what is behind and straining towards what is ahead, I press on towards the goal to win the prize for which God has called me heavenwards in Christ Jesus.'

Carl Beech, CEO, Edge Ministries

Day 7

Waiting with patience

A cave was there, and Saul went in to relieve himself. David and his men were far back in the cave. The men said, 'This is the day the Lord spoke of when he said to you, "I will give your enemy into your hands for you to deal with as you wish."' Then David crept up unnoticed and cut off a corner of Saul's robe.

Afterwards, David was conscience-stricken for having cut off a corner of his robe. He said to his men, 'The Lord forbid that I should do such a thing to my master, the Lord's anointed, or lay my hand on him; for he is the anointed of the Lord.'

1 SAMUEL 24:3–6

Reflection

This might seem like an unusual passage to choose, and yet it has a message for us. How many of us are experiencing times of adversity – and how easy it is to fall into the trap of taking matters into our own hands in order to escape them.

David had already been told that he was going to be king one day, and anointed for that purpose (1 Samuel 16), yet he didn't gain the throne immediately (2 Samuel 5). Although he had always served Saul, the current king, faithfully, David ended up running from him, as Saul was trying to kill him.

David took to the hills, and hid in caves. But, although he was living in basic, difficult circumstances, he still drew followers to himself – in 1 Samuel 22:1–2 we read that 400 men had joined him. By 1 Samuel 23:13 that number had risen to 600. God was working on David's leadership qualities in the secret, hidden places. Do we wait for recognition from others, or for circumstances to seem appropriate before stepping into all God has for us? Do we perhaps hinder the preparation process God is trying to outwork in us, and thereby unintentionally prolong our own waiting? It is worth considering what our attitude is to the circumstances we find ourselves in.

Even though David was being told by those around him that God had obviously delivered Saul into his hands, in his heart he knew that it wasn't the right time. He may have listened to them for a moment, and taken action he regretted, but he was tuned into God's heart enough to recognise that, and humble enough even to apologise to the man who was trying to take his life!

I wonder: whose voices are we listening to in our times of waiting? We may not face such an obvious adversary or be physically on the run, but the difficulties and obstacles in our lives may be used by God to prepare us for some future purpose. Are we prepared to be patient and humble enough to be moulded by him?

Prayer

Lord, I am challenged by David's attitude and actions even when it seemed you had opened up a way out of his difficulties. Help me not to be swayed by others, but to turn to you for direction – and a sense of peace in the waiting.

Jesus Christ the apple tree

The tree of life my soul hath seen,
laden with fruit and always green;
the trees of nature fruitless be,
compared with Christ the apple tree.

His beauty doth all things excel,
by faith I know but ne'er can tell
the glory which I now can see,
in Jesus Christ the apple tree.

For happiness I long have sought,
and pleasure dearly I have bought;
I missed of all: but now I see
'tis found in Christ the apple tree.

I'm weary with my former toil,
here I will sit and rest awhile:
under the shadow I will be,
Of Jesus Christ the apple tree.

This fruit doth make my
      soul to thrive,
it keeps my dying faith alive;
which makes my soul in haste to be
with Jesus Christ the apple tree.

Words attributed to Richard Hutchins,
18th century; composers include
Elizabeth Poston (1905–87)

In a candlelit cathedral, the voices of two or three choristers are lifted in unison, the plaintive music of Elizabeth Poston echoing through the dark corners of the building, a strange contrast to the exuberance of the flowers and decorations which surround the listening congregation.

The carol progresses; more voices are added as the rest of the choristers join in, followed by the deeper harmonies bringing a rich darkness to the melody. The music is aptly suited to the words of these 18th-century lyrics – the voice of someone who has tasted all the world has to offer and found it wanting, finally drawn back to the pure sweetness of the fruit of Christ the apple tree.

For me, this carol is a reminder of the purpose of the incarnation: to rescue humanity from the darkness of sin, to provide a path through to eternity by the grace of Jesus Christ. It may sit oddly among the cheerful sounds of carolling, but the message of hope and love is deeply joyful and profoundly satisfying, making our souls thrive – the fruit of Jesus Christ the apple tree.

Sally Welch, diocesan canon, Christ Church Cathedral, Oxford

Day 8

Preparing the way

A nd you, my child, will be called a prophet of the Most High;
   for you will go on before the Lord to prepare the way for him,
to give his people the knowledge of salvation
   through the forgiveness of their sins,
because of the tender mercy of our God.

LUKE 1:76–78

A voice of one calling:
'In the wilderness prepare
   the way for the Lord;
make straight in the desert
   a highway for our God.'

ISAIAH 40:3

Reflection

John's mother, Elizabeth, received her own miracle around the same time as Mary – an older woman who was barren, she was still a faithful follower and God granted her miracle. That miracle child was the one called to herald Jesus' coming. Her husband, Zechariah, prophesied at John's birth, and our passage from Luke forms part of that prophecy.

As I read this, I am reminded of the significance of the words we speak over our children – whether biologically ours or those within our churches. We need to speak God's life into them and encourage them. There is so much pressure on their generation; we need to be the ones that help them to see God's call upon their lives and lead them towards Jesus.

John himself referred back to Isaiah 40 when he spoke to the crowds in Matthew 3. He knew his calling – but it wasn't an easy one. Living in the desert would have been harsh, and he was also separated from most people. Prophets often did that purposefully so that they could focus themselves on God rather than being distracted by politics and everyday life.

We can view the desert or wilderness as those difficult times in our lives too; how do we prepare a way for God in such seasons? Do we have open hearts towards him, or is our response to struggles to shut him out? Are we open to him working in the midst of hardship in our lives? Sometimes, perhaps, he may allow those moments to stop us from being distracted by worldly things. Do we believe that God can shine his light through us even in those times?

John had an unusual, intense and challenging calling. While many were drawn to hear his message, he was also seen as strange – and a nuisance by religious leaders and Herod. We can be received in a similar way, as our message of gospel hope can be viewed by many as irrelevant in this sophisticated culture of ours. We need to continue, undeterred, to prepare the way for others to receive Jesus.

Prayer

God, I thank you that you call each one of us, and task us with sharing the good news about Jesus to those around us. Help me to be willing to shine your light to everyone I encounter and interact with today.

O come, all ye faithful

O come, all ye faithful,
joyful and triumphant!
O come ye, O come ye,
to Bethlehem!
Come and behold him,
born the king of angels.
O come, let us adore him,
O come, let us adore him,
O come, let us adore him,
Christ the Lord!

God of God, light of light,
lo, he abhors not
the virgin's womb.
Very God,
begotten, not created.
O come, let us adore him,
O come, let us adore him,
O come, let us adore him,
Christ the Lord!

Sing, choirs of angels,
sing in exultation,
sing, all ye citizens
of heaven above!
Glory to God,
all glory in the highest.
O come, let us adore him,
O come, let us adore him,
O come, let us adore him,
Christ the Lord!

Yea, Lord, we greet thee,
born this happy morning,
Jesus, to thee be glory given.
Word of the Father
now in flesh appearing.
O come, let us adore him,
O come, let us adore him,
O come, let us adore him,
Christ the Lord!

John Francis Wade (1711–86)

My heart swells with joy when I hear the chorus of this carol: 'O come, let us adore him, Christ the Lord!' It stirs up deep love, reverence and gratitude within me for God who sent his Son to be with us, our light in the darkness.

Leoné Martin, associate pastor, Cannon Street Memorial Baptist Church, Birmingham

My favourite Christmas hymn is the classic, 'O come, all ye faithful'. This hymn is dear to my heart because of the associations with my family growing up, especially with my dad but also my sister, who died 37 years ago. I have one of those precious, cotton-wool memories of riding in the back-seat of the Chevy my parents had. We were rarely out after dark, so riding back from a work Christmas party my dad took us to, clutching the gift of doll's furniture we'd been given, Judy and I had our noses pressed to the glass as we gazed at what stars could be seen. Dad had taught us to sing this carol in Latin, *Adeste Fideles*, and that's what we were doing, over and over again. (Possibly he regretted having taught it to us…) Years later, on my first Christmas away from home, I stood in a choir on Christmas Eve and choked back tears as I tried to sing the familiar words (in English). Now when I sing it, I love the line 'Sing, all ye citizens of heaven above'. It unites me with Judy and Dad as I think of them, now citizens of heaven above, singing in exultation: 'O come, let us adore him!'

Michele D. Morrison, writer and editor

Day 9

A focused heart

There was also a prophet, Anna, the daughter of Penuel, of the tribe of Asher. She was very old; she had lived with her husband seven years after her marriage, and then was a widow until she was eighty-four. She never left the temple but worshipped night and day, fasting and praying. Coming up to them at that very moment, she gave thanks to God and spoke about the child to all who were looking forward to the redemption of Jerusalem.

LUKE 2:36–38

Reflection

We often include the shepherds and wise men in our Christmas readings, and yet Anna was one who saw the young Jesus too, and she has much to teach us.

Anna experienced bereavement when she became a widow after just seven years, and yet we are told she continually worshipped, prayed and fasted. Like Simeon, who is mentioned in the verses prior to this passage, she is described as a prophet, and I am sure she would have been aware of the fact that Simeon had been promised that he wouldn't die before seeing the Messiah (see Luke 2:26). I imagine she was expectant of seeing the Messiah too as a result. And she is now in our Bibles as one of the first people to spread the news of Jesus' coming – what an honour!

We know that we are often called to wait in patient expectation. But where do we 'live' when we are waiting? Particularly when we have no idea how long we will be waiting for? Do we tend to focus on the one thing we are crying out for, or do we live in a way that reveals we value the presence of God above everything else?

At times, I have given up on spiritual disciplines when life has simply felt too hard and I have had no energy left. And yet I also know what a trap that can be, as prayer and worship hold such power and lift my spirit as well as my gaze. I have been drawn back to fasting again recently, as I pray for breakthrough in particular situations. Jesus himself said, 'When you fast' (Matthew 6:16), so it is clear that he expects us to.

If fasting is not a part of your life right now, can I encourage you to try it – even during the Christmas season? I often fast just one meal – and you can fast from things other than food too (particularly if there are specific reasons why it would be unwise to abstain from food).

Let's take a moment to reflect on what Anna's response was once she had seen the child – she thanked God. We will look at living with a grateful attitude in a later entry; for now can I simply ask: how often do you forget to thank God when you do receive the answers you have been longing for?

Prayer

Today, Lord, help me to be as focused on you as Anna was.

O worship the Lord

O worship the Lord in the beauty of holiness;
bow down before him, his glory proclaim;
with gold of obedience, and incense of lowliness,
kneel and adore him: the Lord is his name.

Low at his feet lay thy burden of carefulness:
high on his heart he will bear it for thee,
comfort thy sorrows, and answer thy prayerfulness,
guiding thy steps as may best for thee be.

Fear not to enter his courts in the slenderness
of the poor wealth thou wouldst reckon as thine:
truth in its beauty, and love in its tenderness,
these are the offerings to lay on his shrine.

These, though we bring them in trembling and fearfulness,
he will accept for the name that is dear;
mornings of joy give for evenings of tearfulness,
trust for our trembling and hope for our fear.

O worship the Lord in the beauty of holiness;
bow down before him, his glory proclaim;
with gold of obedience, and incense of lowliness,
kneel and adore him: the Lord is his name.

John S.B. Monsell (1811–75); composers include
Johann Heinrich Reinhardt (1687–1766)

I offer 'O worship the Lord in the beauty of holiness'. The words remind me that worship lifts us out of the mundane to a sense of wonder and awe. The gifts the wise men brought are gifts we all have: gold, our potential; incense, our prayerfulness; myrrh, soothing healing for pain, ours and others – all accepted by God and used to transform us into the people God knows we can be.

Ann Lewin, poet, author and speaker

Day 10

Permission to be honest

As she kept on praying to the Lord, Eli observed her mouth. Hannah was praying in her heart, and her lips were moving but her voice was not heard. Eli thought she was drunk and said to her, 'How long are you going to stay drunk? Put away your wine.'

'Not so, my lord,' Hannah replied, 'I am a woman who is deeply troubled. I have not been drinking wine or beer; I was pouring out my soul to the Lord. Do not take your servant for a wicked woman; I have been praying here out of my great anguish and grief.'

1 SAMUEL 1:12–16

Reflection

Just because the Christmas season is upon us, it does not mean that our difficult circumstances have melted away, and so I wanted to take some time for us to acknowledge that.

In today's passage we see the childless Hannah in deep distress. I know there will be those reading this who have experienced, and may still be experiencing, the intense heartbreak of childlessness. I pray that you may know God's comfort and care in such a difficult time.

Whatever particular grief or anguish you may be experiencing, know that you can take your pain and your tears and pour it all out before God. Here we see a woman unafraid to 'ugly cry' in front of her God – and anyone else watching. Passages such as this one in the Bible reassure me that God is not afraid of emotional outbursts – in fact he encourages these when necessary.

There have been moments in recent years where the extraordinary depths of pain and grief have wracked my body and soul, and I have been unable to do anything but sob my heart out. I have had to make the choice either to do that before my God or try to hide from him. In all honesty, there have been moments of both – although I know he always sees me. But when I have come before him, I have certainly felt less alone.

The hardest thing can be when we are misunderstood in our grief – and in our waiting – as Hannah was. How difficult she must have found it that the man of God assumed she was drunk! But even other well-meaning Christians can say and do similar things to us when they misread situations or our behaviour. That can cause us to question ourselves, and God, but it is important to remember that God's heart is always tender towards us. Let's not allow our responses to be based on our treatment from others. Like Hannah, we know in our hearts whether we have become bitter or if we are staying soft towards God. However painful it is right now, let's keep our eyes fixed on God.

Prayer

Lord, I am grateful for the example of those, like Hannah, who poured out their anguish readily before you. Help me to be open to you about all my thoughts and feelings.

The amber beads

They are so smooth as I turn them
in my hand
The amber beads
Save for that little nick
Just there
Where they caught on your
little teeth
As I pushed them in your mouth
to hush you
As we ran through that night
so long ago.

As I warm them in my hand
I remember my friend, Milkah,
Handing them to you to
Soothe your aching gums
As you played with her Simon
in the courtyard.

Milkah and Simon
Both murdered
When she would not give
Her baby up to the soldiers.
So many little ones
All dead.

We survived
Perhaps because the precious beads
Kept you from whimpering in fear
As we slunk away through the night.

I later heard that they
Were looking for you
As they ruthlessly slaughtered
Every boy child under the age of two.

So is it our fault
That they died,
Even as we survived?

My mind tells me
It was down to Herod's
Envy and fear of a
Two-year-old.
Tyrants have no rationality
And no mercy

But as I rub the amber beads
My heart aches
For my friend and her little one.
Could we have somehow saved
her and Simon?
And what of the others?

I see you hanging there
in the place of execution
And I wonder if
This other Herod smirks to himself
That he got you after all.

But he didn't
I know now that
Your life and your death
Have been a purposeful sacrifice
To save us all

Giving meaning to all who have
ever suffered
And I rub the amber beads
In thanksgiving for
Milkah and Simon
Who helped to save you
To meet this hour.

Rachele Vernon O'Brien

'The amber beads' is a poem linking Mary's reflections on the massacre of the Holy Innocents, when Herod ordered the slaughter of all the boy babies in Bethlehem under two, with the crucifixion. It reminds us that Jesus probably played with some of these children and that Mary may well have known some of the mothers. It looks at survivor's guilt. In writing this poem, I wished to honour those who every day fly from tyranny with young children.

Rachele Vernon O'Brien, theologian and Anglican deacon

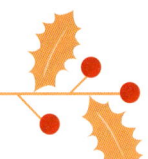

Joy

Child in the manger

Child in the manger,
infant of Mary;
outcast and stranger,
Lord of all;
child who inherits
all our transgressions,
all our demerits
on him fall.

Once the most holy
child of salvation
gently and lowly
lived below;
now as our glorious
mighty Redeemer,
see him victorious
o'er each foe.

Prophets foretold him,
infant of wonder;
angels behold him
on his throne;
worthy our Saviour
of all their praises;
happy forever
are his own.

Mary Macdonald (1789–1872), translated by Lachlan Macbean (1853–1931)

I love this carol for a number of reasons. Firstly, because it was written by a Baptist, Gaelic-speaking female poet on the island of Mull at a time when the dominant Presbyterian culture in Scotland discouraged the celebration of Christmas. Mary MacDonald wrote it to a tune which she heard from a travelling fiddler who was playing in the village of Bunessan. This tune was consequently poached from its original text and associated with the more popular text, 'Morning has broken'. Secondly, I love it because it is completely lacking any of the mawkish sentiment of so many Christmas carols, which say things which are completely unbiblical, such as Jesus being a baby who never cried. Rather, MacDonald depends on scriptural imagery for her text. And thirdly, it bears witness to the sacred scandal of the incarnation, namely that the God who is all-powerful should come, out of compassion and in solidarity with humanity, to be one of us and redeem us not from above, but from below.

John L. Bell, hymn writer, broadcaster and member of the Iona Community

Day 11

Filled with the Holy Spirit

When Elizabeth heard Mary's greeting, the baby leaped in her womb, and Elizabeth was filled with the Holy Spirit. In a loud voice she exclaimed: 'Blessed are you among women, and blessed is the child you will bear! But why am I so favoured, that the mother of my Lord should come to me? As soon as the sound of your greeting reached my ears, the baby in my womb leaped for joy.'

LUKE 1:41–44

Reflection

We are returning today to the start of the Christmas story. There is much joy within the interaction between the relatives Elizabeth and Mary. Both were pregnant miraculously, and both knew that their children were gifts from God. But I want to focus on John for a moment. He was a baby still in the womb, and yet his response to Mary's arrival was to leap for joy! We are also told that at that exact moment 'Elizabeth was filled with the Holy Spirit' – the two things seemed to go hand in hand.

We know that one of the fruits of the Spirit is joy (see Galatians 5:22–23); it is beautiful to see here how the Holy Spirit touched both Elizabeth and the baby growing inside her. Somehow, John recognised the presence of Jesus inside Mary and it caused a leap of joy. Elizabeth, too, could see with spiritual eyes that Mary was 'the mother of my Lord'. That can only be the Holy Spirit's doing!

I am challenged when I read this passage. We can become so overfamiliar with the Christmas narrative that the details simply wash over us. And yet here an unborn baby responded with a joyful leap! There seems to have been so much meaning wrapped up in that leap – including all the hopes and longings of the whole Old Testament. We can forget that there was a period of 400 years between the Old and New Testaments; an extended time of waiting, and hoping, for the promised Messiah. May we not forget the intensity of emotions wrapped up in that – and then the incredible joy of knowing the Messiah was on the way.

That same Messiah is the one we are able to converse with every day; who has called us his sisters and brothers. Take some time to ponder that truth today.

It's also worth noticing how full of joy Elizabeth was for Mary. Interestingly, even though she was finally pregnant herself and therefore could have felt that her situation was being overshadowed by Mary's, she was generous and welcoming. She could have been jealous, but there seems no hint of that here. When we allow the Spirit's joy to flood us, it affects our everyday interactions too.

Prayer

Lord, help me to be filled with wonder afresh today at the story of your coming.

Adam lay abounden

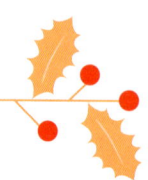

Adam lay abounden, bounden in a bond
Four thousand winters thought he not too long.

And all was for an apple, an apple that he took,
As clerks find written in there book.

Ne'er had the apple taken been, the apple taken been
Ne'er had never our Lady have been heaven's queen.

Blessed be the time that apple taken was
Therefore we must sing 'Deo gratias!'

Medieval, translated by Emma Pennington

There are some pieces of music and words which we only hear around the Christmas period and this wonderful medieval poem is one of them. It's always been a favourite of mine, whether set to music by Peter Warlock or Boris Ord or even embedded into the 'A Ceremony of Carols' by Benjamin Britten because of its strong link with our medieval heritage. It dates from the 15th century and can be found in a manuscript in the British Library along with a number of other songs that could well have been sung by a minstrel.

And this is why I like it so much, because it manages to express a complex theological doctrine in a simple yet humorous way that could be remembered and sung again by whoever heard it.

In a traditional Christmas carol service, the anthem 'Adam lay abounden' is often paired with the story of the fall because this is what it essentially is about. In medieval theology when Adam died, like all the patriarchs, it was believed that he was unable to go to heaven and was held in a state of limbo until the crucifixion of Christ when the bonds of death and sin were broken. By medieval reckoning it was calculated as a period of 4,000 winters. In this cheeky song, the great deeds of the fall are presented as nothing more than a naughty schoolboy's stealing of an apple. But it is because of this that we have our subsequent redemption through the incarnation of Jesus Christ.

So the poem captures the sweep of redemption history and the wonderfully positive doctrine of the happy fault, *felix culpa*, which was first set out by Thomas Aquinas in the 13th century. It's the way this poem expresses in very human and simple terms those complex doctrines which reveal that even sin may have a place in the great scheme of God's plan that so speaks to me at a time of peace, forgiveness and love.

Emma Pennington, canon missioner, Canterbury Cathedral

Day 12

A different kind of joy

Weeping may stay for the night,
    but rejoicing comes in the morning.
When I felt secure, I said,
    'I shall never be shaken.'
Lord, when you favoured me,
    you made my royal mountain stand firm;
but when you hid your face,
    I was dismayed.
To you, Lord, I called;
    to the Lord I cried for mercy…
You turned my wailing into dancing;
    you removed my sackcloth and clothed me with joy,
that my heart may sing your praises and not be silent.
    Lord my God, I will praise you forever.

PSALM 30:5–8, 11–12

Reflection

It can be difficult to think about joy when we are going through testing times. I have wrestled with God about this myself and am now convinced there is a joy that surpasses our earthly circumstances that God wants us to experience. One of the ways that we tap into it is through honest conversation with him.

In my own struggles I have often turned to the psalms, particularly those written by David. His writing, like the story of Hannah (see day 10), seems to give us permission to be honest. David is upfront about his emotions, his circumstances and his questions – but also speaks to his soul and acknowledges the sovereignty of God. He often turns to worship even in the midst of lament, which is something I have learned to do.

So much in our world has been shaken in recent years and for those of us who have lived in relative safety and prosperity, it has been a shock. In this psalm, David reflects on how invincible he had felt when everything was going well; it is all too easy to forget to rely on God when all seems to be ticking along fine. Pain reminds us to cry out to him.

David faced a range of highs and lows in his life – a successful king, he also had moments when he had to run for his life and when he endured God's judgement. So his line 'Weeping may stay for the night, but rejoicing comes in the morning' seems to hold a wider, eternal perspective.

In 2 Corinthians 4:16–17, Paul said: 'Though outwardly we are wasting away, yet inwardly we are being renewed day by day. For our light and momentary troubles are achieving for us an eternal glory that far outweighs them all.' This was a scripture my mum used to reach for again and again – she suffered physical pain for decades and eventually we watched her 'waste away'. But her faith never did.

Even in the midst of difficulties, God can turn our 'wailing into dancing'. It seems like an utter mystery to me at times, but I know the truth of this. Whether it is you or someone you know who is in a season of weeping, cry out to God for his mercy.

Prayer

Lord, thank you that you do clothe us with joy. May I experience your supernatural joy today.

Sussex Carol

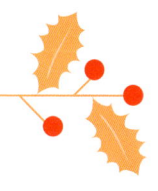

On Christmas night all Christians sing
To hear the news the angels bring

News of great joy, news of great mirth
News of our merciful King's birth

Then why should men on earth be so sad,
Since our Redeemer made us glad,

When from our sin he set us free,
All for to gain our liberty?

When sin departs before His grace
Then life and health come in its place

Angels and men with joy may sing
All for to see the newborn king.

All out of darkness we have light,
Which made the angels sing this night

'Glory to God and peace to men
Now and forevermore, Amen!'

Words by Luke Wadding (1588–1657); music by Vaughan Williams (1872–1958),
among others

A delight for me at Christmas is Vaughan Williams' 'Fantasia on Christmas Carols', which over the years I have sung with different choirs. Set to sublime music, the three carols tell the Christian/human story, beginning with creation and the fall, telling the Christmas story with a refrain of Mary praying that includes the 'Sussex Carol', sharing the joyful good news of Jesus to all people, regardless of their circumstances.

Lakshmi Jeffreys, rector, St George the Martyr Church, Wootton

Day 13

Rejoicing in God's rescue plan

W as it not you who dried up the sea,
the waters of the great deep,
who made a road in the depths of the sea
so that the redeemed might cross over?
Those the Lord has rescued will return.
They will enter Zion with singing;
everlasting joy will crown their heads.
Gladness and joy will overtake them,
and sorrow and sighing will flee away.

ISAIAH 51:10–11

For he remembered his holy promise
given to his servant Abraham.
He brought out his people with rejoicing,
his chosen ones with shouts of joy.

PSALM 105:42–43

81

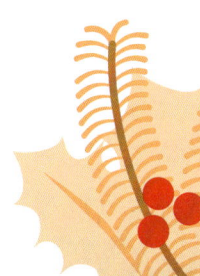

Reflection

Both these passages reflect back on a time of miraculous deliverance: the parting of the Red Sea so that the Israelites could escape slavery in Egypt. What did the multitudes who crossed that sea and saw their enemies engulfed by it do straight afterwards? They worshipped. Moses and Miriam led them all in songs of deliverance (see Exodus 15), declaring what God had done for them and how incredible he is. As we saw with David, singing seems to be closely linked with the gift of joy. The Israelites had just escaped their enemies, and yet they hadn't entered the promised land. They must have been aware that they had a challenging time ahead of them, but still chose to take time out to rejoice in the freedom God had brought them.

The passage in Isaiah was spoken at a time when God's people were again facing exile and captivity. There is much in the prophet's words that speaks of God's judgement against them for their unfaithfulness, but he was also the one who spoke the most about the coming Messiah – the one who would be raised up to deliver them and provide everlasting joy. It is so incredible to look back and read the words of Isaiah knowing the story of Jesus and what he has done for us all. At the time, they were eagerly awaiting this promised Messiah; in this season we can rejoice in the fact that we know who he is and have experienced the deliverance and freedom that his coming to earth provided for us.

Just a few chapters later, in Isaiah 53, the prophet describes Jesus in incredible detail, including the purpose he was born on earth for. It is mind-blowing to pause and ponder how the story of the Bible fits together. This Old Testament prophet would have had no concept of Jesus dying for our sins – in those days unblemished lambs had to be sacrificed regularly – and yet he spoke of the one 'led like a lamb to the slaughter' (Isaiah 53:7). God rescued his people again and again, and then provided the ultimate rescue through his Son Jesus. How incredible!

Prayer

God, when I ponder the stories of rescue in the Bible, and reflect on Jesus' ultimate rescue plan, I can't help but rejoice in the salvation you have provided.

The holy city

Last night I lay a sleeping,
There came a dream so fair,
I stood in old Jerusalem
Beside the temple there.
I heard the children singing,
And ever as they sang,
Methought the voice of angels
From heav'n in answer rang;
Methought the voice of angels
From heav'n in answer rang:
Jerusalem! Jerusalem!
Lift up your gates and sing,
Hosanna in the highest
Hosanna to your king!

And then methought my dream
    was changed,
The streets no longer rang,
Hushed were the glad hosannas
The little children sang.

The sun grew dark with mystery,
The morn was cold and chill,
As the shadow of a cross arose
Upon a lonely hill,
As the shadow of a cross arose
Upon a lonely hill.
Jerusalem! Jerusalem!
Hark! how the angels sing,
Hosanna in the highest,
Hosanna to your king.

And once again the scene was changed,
New earth there seem'd to be,
I saw the holy city
Beside the tideless sea;
The light of God was on its streets,
The gates were open wide,
And all who would might enter,
And no one was denied.

No need of moon or stars by night,
Or sun to shine by day,
It was the new Jerusalem,
That would not pass away,
It was the new Jerusalem,
That would not pass away.

Words by Frederic Weatherly (1848–1929); music by Michael Maybrick (alias Stephen Adams; 1841–1913)

When I was a little girl, my father used to play this music, along with my other favourite, 'O holy night', on Christmas Eve on our ancient wind-up gramophone. I fell asleep with this music ringing in my ears. Sixty years later I was stopped in my tracks, while navigating a large international airport in a non-Christian country just before Christmas, when, to my amazed delight, this same music rang out over the PA system. I was transported right back to childhood Christmases. Music transcends all our borders, faith systems and time periods, and for this precious moment, in transit in an alien environment, it held for me the power to transfigure *every* city and *every* night, into holiness.

Margaret Silf, author and speaker

Day 14

A joy that lasts

The word of the Lord spread through the whole region. But the Jewish leaders… stirred up persecution against Paul and Barnabas… So they shook the dust off their feet as a warning to them and went to Iconium. And the disciples were filled with joy and with the Holy Spirit.

ACTS 13:49–52

Let us run with perseverance the race marked out for us, fixing our eyes on Jesus… For the joy that was set before him he endured the cross, scorning its shame, and sat down at the right hand of the throne of God. Consider him who endured such opposition from sinners, so that you will not grow weary and lose heart.

HEBREWS 12:1–3

Reflection

At Christmas we usually spend time focusing on cosy images of the baby Jesus surrounded by his parents and animals. We've already considered how that is a sanitised version of events, but I want us to take time now to reflect on the fact that Jesus chose to come to earth as a helpless baby precisely because he knew he would provide our only means of salvation. He understood his time of ministering as a human would end in a horrific death. But 'for the joy that was set before him he endured the cross' (Hebrews 12:2). What was that joy? I believe it was his future radiant bride, the church, being able to draw close to him without sin's blemish. How incredible is that?

In Acts 13 we read of how Paul and Barnabas travelled around, spreading the good news. But sometimes they came up against ridicule and opposition. What did they do? They shook the dust off their feet and moved on to the next place, undeterred. We are also told that the disciples were 'filled with joy and with the Holy Spirit' (v. 52). Even in the midst of persecution we can learn to fix our eyes on Jesus and know his joy.

Recently, I heard the testimony of a man who had converted from Islam to Christianity while on pilgrimage to Mecca. As a result of that decision, he shared that his family disowned him, he was forcibly divorced from his wife and his children were taken from him. He has since relocated to England, where he tells others about Jesus, both in person and online. When asked how he coped with the intense pain of all he has faced, he said that his joy is in seeing others saved.

All these examples are huge provocations to me. It is easy to get caught up in our own day-to-day experiences and forget to share the good news that we already know. This year, why not take time to stop and ponder the joy of your salvation afresh – and ask God for opportunities to share it with others. As we are encouraged to in 1 Peter 3:15: 'Always be prepared to give an answer to everyone who asks you to give the reason for the hope that you have'.

Prayer

Lord, help me not to grow weary. Revive in me again the joy of knowing you – and help me to share that joy with those around me.

God's grandeur

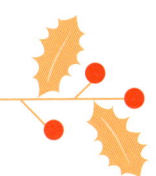

The world is charged with the grandeur of God.
    It will flame out, like shining from shook foil;
    It gathers to a greatness, like the ooze of oil
Crushed. Why do men then now not reck his rod?
Generations have trod, have trod, have trod;
    And all is seared with trade; bleared, smeared with toil;
    And wears man's smudge and shares man's smell: the soil
Is bare now, nor can foot feel, being shod.

And for all this, nature is never spent;
    There lives the dearest freshness deep down things;
And though the last lights off the black West went
    Oh, morning, at the brown brink eastward, springs –
Because the Holy Ghost over the bent
    World broods with warm breast and with ah! bright wings.

Gerard Manley Hopkins (1844–89)

In this short poem, Manley Hopkins threads a needle through toil and thwarted human ambition towards grace and redemption. 'Generations have trod, have trod, have trod', seeking their own path – their own soil apart from God. But he – and his grace – are inescapable. The whole of creation is charged with it, the ever renewing and revitalising pregnancy of nature a constant whispering to humankind that his mercies are new each morning. Nature itself, then, is an avatar for the grand narrative wired into the cosmos: mercy and new life might just be behind the next rock.

Andy Kind, comedian, preacher and writer

Day 15

Cultivating gratitude

Rejoice always, pray continually, give thanks in all circumstances; for this is God's will for you in Christ Jesus.

Do not quench the Spirit. Do not treat prophecies with contempt but test them all; hold on to what is good, reject every kind of evil.

May God himself, the God of peace, sanctify you through and through. May your whole spirit, soul and body be kept blameless at the coming of our Lord Jesus Christ. The one who calls you is faithful, and he will do it.

1 THESSALONIANS 5:16–24

Reflection

The Christmas season often appears full of jollity. We sing carols with gusto and enjoy laughter with friends and family. And yet the joy that we find in God transcends all seasons and circumstances. The joy of our salvation can hold us even in moments of weeping.

I used to read the start of our passage with incredulity. How can we rejoice at all times and give thanks in every circumstance? And yet I think the key to that is being in prayer – in conversation – with God throughout our days. The instruction is not to be grateful 'for' but 'in' all circumstances – there is a big difference. And gratitude is in itself a key to unlocking joy. This is something that mental health experts are recognising; many encourage the practice of finding three things to be grateful for each day. Practising this regularly actually rewires our brains, helping us to be more content.

What we focus on and the words that we speak out have a huge bearing on our emotions. I am not one who only allows positive confession out of my mouth; I believe it is important to be honest about where we are at, both in the good times and the bad. However, I have been talking to our teenagers about making the choice to look beyond the negative. We can pray and ask God to open our eyes to all he is doing around us each day – there is much to be grateful for even in the little details.

As a family we also practise gratitude at the end of each day; it has become a part of our bedtime routine, something we do together before turning the lights out.

This passage instructs us to be proactive in all areas of our lives, and reminds us that the spiritual realm is as real as the physical and we need to be wise and discerning. It also gives us the much-needed reminders that God is faithful, and Jesus *is* coming again.

This Christmas, let us take the time to slow down, notice and thank God for all the ways he is at work in our lives each day.

Prayer

Lord Jesus, I thank you that you are active in my life today; open my eyes to see what you are doing. And help me to cultivate a thankful attitude.

In dulci jubilo

In dulci jubilo
  Let us our homage shew:
  Our heart's joy reclineth
In praesepio;
  And like a bright star shineth
Matris in gremio,
Alpha es et O!
Alpha es et O!

O Jesu parvule,
  My heart is sore for Thee!
  Hear me, I beseech Thee,
O puer optime;
  My praying let it reach Thee,
O princeps gloriae.
Trahe me post te.
Trahe me post te.

O patris caritas!
O Nati lenitas!
    Deeply were we stained.
Per nostra crimina:
    But Thou for us hast gained
Coelorum gaudia,
Qualis gloria!
Qualis gloria!

Ubi sunt gaudia,
    If that they be not there?
    There are Angels singing
Nova cantica;
    And there the bells are ringing
In Regis curia.
    O that we were there!
    O that we were there!

Robert Pearsall (1795–1856)

Did you know that a 'macaronic' carol is one sung in more than one language? They were popular in early medieval times, when Latin was used in church and the Bible was mainly learnt and quoted in Latin, too. In Christmas carols, though, church Latin and the spoken language of the people mingled together, and must have sounded like heaven meeting earth: the song of the angels heard and repeated in the voices of the shepherds. 'In dulci jubilo' is a particularly good example, given the legends surrounding its composition: angels are supposed to have invited the mystic Heinrich Seuse to join them in a dance, and this is what they were singing. A favourite tale from my childhood tells of Brother Heinrich writing down the tune, but forgetting how it ended, and his donkey joining in with an enthusiastic 'Hee-haw!' which can be heard in the repeat of the final line.

The great thing about a macaronic carol is that even though the English lines have been translated from the medieval German, and change across the versions, the Latin lines are the same words that were sung in the 14th century. When I sing it or hear it, I think of my Christmas rejoicing linked across centuries and across countries, with a cloud of witnesses and angels – and perhaps even one donkey.

Amy Scott Robinson, author and storyteller

Peace

I saw it standing still

But I myself, Joseph, was walking, and I was not walking. I looked up to the celestial sphere of heaven, and I saw it standing still, and into the air and I saw it frozen, and the birds of the sky were still. And I looked down to the earth, and I saw a bowl set for workers who were reclined to eat, and their hands were in the bowl. And those who were chewing were not chewing, and those who were taking from the bowl were not lifting up, and those who were bringing food to their mouths were not bringing food to their mouths. Rather all their faces were looking up. And I saw sheep being herded, but the sheep stood still. And the shepherd had raised his hand to strike them, but his hand stood in the air. And I looked down at the flow of the river, and I saw goats, and their mouths were suspended over the water, but they were not drinking. And all of a sudden, all things returned to their course.

Protoevangelium of James 18:2

This reflection from the non-canonical infancy gospel of James describes time standing still when Jesus was born. Matthew has the star of the east stand still over the place of Jesus' birth (Matthew 2:9; likely the star of Numbers 24:17). We often speak of momentous occasions as moments when time stands still – it is as if everything in life freezes, so that we might inhale the moment, experience it in all its depth and for that moment think of nothing else. These can be moments of joy or moments of horror; invariably, they mark our consciousness forever. The thought of such moments may come and go, but never go away. In many respects, these moments shape our identity and the way that we view the world.

When I reflect on the birth of the Messiah, I want to embrace this moment when time stood still. Who I am is indelibly shaped by the notion that the creator God visited the earth and set about the plan of rebuilding and restoring the beauty and perfection of the original creation. I am moulded by the fact that he did this without violence or armies, without riches or political influence, without bullying anyone or trying to exert his superiority. He was as humble in life and death as was pre-empted in his humble birth.

Christmas strikes me as a time, aided perhaps by its location towards the end of a year, where we do well to allow time to stand still for a moment, so we may reassess our priorities, rethink our agendas, reflect on our successes and failures and recommit ourselves to the values championed in the Messiah's life. In the narrative of the first Joshua, time stood still that Israel could be victorious (Joshua 10:12–13). In the narrative of the birth of the Great Joshua (Joshua=Yeshua=Jesus), time stood still so that through the one who embodied the true Israel, the whole world could experience victory.

Andrew Boakye, lecturer in religions and theology, University of Manchester

Day 16

Quietness and rest

The Lord is my shepherd, I lack nothing.
    He makes me lie down in green pastures,
he leads me beside quiet waters,
    he refreshes my soul.
He guides me along the right paths for his name's sake.
Even though I walk through the darkest valley,
I will fear no evil,
    for you are with me;
your rod and your staff, they comfort me.
You prepare a table before me in the presence of my enemies.
You anoint my head with oil;
    my cup overflows.
Surely your goodness and love will follow me all the days of my life,
and I will dwell in the house of the Lord forever.

PSALM 23

Reflection

As we turn to look at peace, I want us to start by spending time with the incredible imagery within Psalm 23. Though not specifically describing peace, this passage has taught me so much about living a peaceful life with God. It exudes a sense of quietness and rest, as well as abundant provision.

So let's take a moment to press the pause button. Are we getting caught up in the usual rushing about over the festive season? Are we running around trying to provide everything for those we love? Yes, there are things to do, but it is so important to take time to rest in God and be refreshed. He will guide us along the right path; he also has a table prepared for us of all we need each day, and there is more than enough – our cups overflow.

We don't need to buy into our culture's myth of needing more and more stuff – especially at Christmas – for ourselves and our loved ones. And we *can* take time out to intentionally focus on dwelling with God. A few years ago we had a discussion in our church small group about praying a simple prayer each day: 'Lord, please order my day.' Looking to him right at the start of each day, and handing over control of our lives by asking him to order them, has made such a difference to many of us. Doing so has helped to calm me when I've felt overwhelmed by all the tasks ahead of me.

I've also had him prompt me to make time within a busy working day to meet with someone – and then my work has come together so much more quickly than I expected afterwards. I have seen him direct my path and, even though he sometimes takes me a way I'd rather he didn't, I've known his tender care too.

You might want to take a few minutes to visualise the scene of being led to quiet waters and lying down in green pastures and ask Jesus, our good shepherd, for his refreshment.

Prayer

Lord, I thank you that even though there may be lots going on around me, I can take time to pause and rest in your presence. I also hand over the rest of my day to you – please bring your peace and your order to it.

O little town of Bethlehem

O little town of Bethlehem,
How still we see thee lie!
Above thy deep and dreamless sleep
The silent stars go by.
Yet in thy dark streets shineth
The everlasting light;
The hopes and fears of all the years
Are met in thee tonight.

O morning stars together
Proclaim the holy birth!
And praises sing to God the King
And peace to men on earth.
For Christ is born of Mary,
And gathered all above,
While mortals sleep, the angels keep
Their watch of wondering love.

How silently, how silently
The wondrous gift is given
So God imparts to human hearts
The blessings of his heaven
No ear may hear his coming,
But in this world of sin,
Where meek souls will receive
    him still,
The dear Christ enters in.

O holy child of Bethlehem,
Descend to us, we pray!
Cast out our sin and enter in,
Be born in us today.
We hear the Christmas angels,
The great glad tidings tell;
O come to us, abide with us,
Our Lord Emmanuel!

Words by Phillips Brooks (1835–93);
music by Vaughan Williams (1872–1958)

My favourite Christmas carol is 'O little town of Bethlehem'. I love the sense of God coming softly, unannounced, and the reminder for us today to look in unremarkable places in order to find the extraordinary presence of God. I also find this particularly meaningful since visiting the Holy Land on several occasions and seeing the paradox of Bethlehem today, both a place of pilgrimage, heavy with the story of God, and a town in the West Bank, in the middle of ongoing conflict and pain. Somehow the song captures it all.

Isabelle Hamley, secretary for theology and theological adviser to the House of Bishops

Day 17

A gift from Jesus

These words you hear are not my own; they belong to the Father who sent me. All this I have spoken while still with you. But the Advocate, the Holy Spirit, whom the Father will send in my name, will teach you all things and will remind you of everything I have said to you. Peace I leave with you; my peace I give you. I do not give to you as the world gives. Do not let your hearts be troubled and do not be afraid.

JOHN 14:24–27

Reflection

Today's verses are part of a much longer conversation that Jesus was having with his disciples as he prepared them for what was to happen in the coming days. It is here that he mentions his peace being given to them. Interestingly, he uses the same phrase that the angel of the Lord who spoke to Zechariah, to Mary and to Joseph used: 'Do not be afraid.' So often when God speaks to us about a change of direction – which those characters in the Christmas story certainly were facing – our initial response can be fear; as it can be when we see God moving in ways that we don't understand, which the disciples had been experiencing, and would do in even greater measure. Like Mary, we too can be 'troubled' (Luke 1:29), which God knows. He provides peace in a way that the world does not.

We can view peace as simply the absence of conflict, which is how most dictionaries describe it. We may have witnessed world leaders, government officials and work colleagues try to 'keep the peace' by compromising; this can happen in our homes too. Yet Jesus' peace is different, and we are going to take some time over the next few days to dig deeper into that. For now, I think it comes as a huge reassurance that, just as Jesus explained how the Holy Spirit would come and be the disciples' (and our) counsellor and guide, he also revealed that his peace would be with them too. We do not need to fear the future, or our circumstances, when we experience his peace.

It is important to notice that he says 'I do not give to you as the world gives' (v. 27). So often, gifts come with strings attached. There can be hidden reasons for a gift; perhaps someone is trying to curry favour with us or wants to manipulate us into their way of thinking. Jesus' gift of peace is given freely to us. May we be instruments of his peace this Christmas, as it says in Romans 12:18: 'As far as it depends on you, live at peace with everyone.'

Prayer

Lord Jesus, thank you so much for the gift of peace. I take a moment now to pause and receive it from you afresh today.

Silent night

Silent night, holy night!
All is calm, all is bright
round yon virgin mother and child!
Holy infant, so tender and mild,
sleep in heavenly peace,
sleep in heavenly peace.

Silent night, holy night!
Shepherds quake at the sight.
Glories stream from heaven afar,
heav'nly hosts sing, Alleluia!
Christ, the Saviour, is born!
Christ, the Saviour, is born!

Silent night, holy night!
Son of God, love's pure light
radiant beams from thy holy face
with the dawn of redeeming grace,
Jesus, Lord, at thy birth,
Jesus, Lord, at thy birth.

Words by Joseph Mohr (1792–1848), translated by John Freeman Young (1820–85);
music by Franz Xaver Gruber (1787–1863)

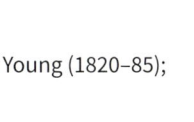

This carol has a particular resonance for me at Christmas because I remember singing it in Polish when I was young (my parents were Polish). I found it very moving then and continue to do so now when I sing it in English. I think this is because I appreciate reflective and quieter worship. I find that this carol particularly speaks to me of God's redeeming grace, thus linking Jesus' incarnation with his death and resurrection. Its quieter melody helps me to reflect on these truths about Jesus: who he is, and what he has done for me through coming into this world as a baby to become my Saviour so that I can know God's redeeming grace.

Meric Srokosz, professor, National Oceanography Centre, and author

My dad was born in Germany in 1909. He came to Britain in his early 20s, as the Nazi grip on power tightened in his homeland; I never really discovered whether he was a political refugee or what is now often called an economic migrant. My childhood Christmas memories include him rather tunelessly singing 'Silent night' in the original German. It was a link with his past, and also (though I doubt he thought of it) of the hardships faced by the child whose birth the carol recounts.

Martin Leckebusch, hymn writer and author

Day 18

Making all things new

Then I saw 'a new heaven and a new earth'... 'God's dwelling-place is now among the people, and he will dwell with them. They will be his people, and God himself will be with them and be their God. "He will wipe every tear from their eyes. There will be no more death" or mourning or crying or pain, for the old order of things has passed away.'

REVELATION 21:1, 3–4

The wolf will live with the lamb,
    the leopard will lie down with the goat,
the calf and the lion and the yearling together;
    and a little child will lead them.

ISAIAH 11:6

111

Reflection

Right at the start of our devotions, we saw Jesus described as 'Prince of Peace', and that 'of the greatness of his government and peace there will be no end' (Isaiah 9:6–7). This prophecy occurred hundreds of years before Jesus came to earth as a baby. The same prophet, Isaiah, is also quoted here where the passage talks about God wiping away our tears (see Isaiah 25:8). In Isaiah 11:1–9 he describes the peace that Jesus will bring, when nature is returned to the harmony it was originally created to have.

During Jesus' time on earth, he was 'establishing and upholding [his kingdom] with justice and righteousness' (Isaiah 9:7), and this continues today. The ultimate picture of God's purposes, and the culmination of the whole of human history, is described in the pictorial language of our passages today. Revelation can be a confusing book, full of strange imagery, and yet it shows Jesus bringing his rule and reign – his peace (*shalom*, which means complete well-being) – once and for all. To bring about such peace, Jesus needs to bring his justice to bear on the world and his enemies, and it is upon this that much of Revelation is centred, as is Isaiah 11:4–5.

As we prepare to celebrate Jesus' coming once again, let us remember the bigger picture. While his coming as a helpless baby can seem like such a strange plan – and many in his day couldn't understand why he didn't come as a warrior leader – ultimately he is the Prince of Peace, and we can look forward to a time when nothing will interrupt the peace he brings.

We have an eternal destiny with Jesus in which all the old order – all the pain, death and mourning – will be no more. What an amazing truth to keep hold of. It is far too easy to look at what is going on in the world today and allow ourselves to be robbed of peace. But ultimately there is a future far beyond what we can imagine now – with the Prince of Peace himself. We need his perspective in our everyday lives; what a difference that makes!

Prayer

Lord Jesus, I thank you that you are the Prince of Peace, and that you are coming again to make all things new. Help me to remember that the whole of history is held in your hands and you are in control. I trust you with my life today.

Hark! The herald angels sing

Hark! The herald angels sing,
'Glory to the newborn king:
peace on earth and mercy mild,
God and sinners reconciled!'
Joyful, all ye nations, rise,
join the triumph of the skies,
with th'angelic host proclaim,
'Christ is born in Bethlehem!'

Hark! The herald angels sing,
'Glory to the newborn king!'

Christ, by highest heaven adored,
Christ, the everlasting Lord,
late in time behold him come,
offspring of the virgin's womb:
veiled in flesh the Godhead see,
hail th'incarnate Deity,
pleased as man with man to dwell,
Jesus, our Immanuel.

Hark! The herald angels sing,
'Glory to the newborn king!'

Hail the heaven-born Prince of Peace!
Hail the Sun of Righteousness!
Light and life to all he brings,
risen with healing in his wings.
Mild he lays his glory by,
born that man no more may die,
born to raise the sons of earth,
born to give them second birth.

Hark! The herald angels sing,
'Glory to the newborn king!'

Words by Charles Wesley (1707–88),
adapted by George Whitefield (1714–70);
music by Felix Mendelssohn (1809–47),
adapted by William Hayman Cummings
(1831–1915)

I love this carol, with its clear proclamation of truth and its call to action. I was thrilled when my fellow journalists at the *Eastbourne Herald* sang it enthusiastically each Christmas, putting the emphasis on the 'herald' while unwittingly declaring 'God and sinners reconciled'! I rejoice at its subliminal prophetic expectation that one day people 'from every nation, tribe, people and language' will stand before the throne and before the Lamb and cry out: 'Salvation belongs to our God' (Revelation 7:9–10). *Maranatha* – come, Lord Jesus.

Catherine Butcher, author, journalist and communications consultant

I must admit that when it comes to Christmas carols, I can quite quickly go into autopilot mode once the season rolls in to start singing them. A while ago, I took it upon myself to really pay attention to the lyrics, and year upon year, I'm always struck by these words from 'Hark! The herald angels sing':

> *Mild he lays his glory by,*
> *born that man no more may die,*
> *born to raise the sons of earth,*
> *born to give them second birth.*

How powerful. What a Saviour!

Naomi Aidoo, coach, author and entrepreneur

You know that old saying, 'If you want something done well, do it yourself'? Well, this carol is proof that real perfection comes with teamwork. When the great Charles Wesley wrote this carol in 1739, the first line was 'Hark how all the welkin rings'. He knew 'welkin' meant the vaults of heaven, but no one else did, so his ministry colleague George Whitefield tactfully changed that first line to 'Hark! The herald angels sing'. Then, 40 years later, when Tate and Brady brought out their new hymnbook, they decided that this carol would be even better with the addition of the chorus that we all now know and love. And Wesley had stipulated that this carol needed stately sombre music – with exactly the same determination as, a century later, Mendelssohn insisted that the melody he wrote to mark the invention of the printing press should *never* be partnered with sacred words. So, both men would have turned in their graves to know that, 15 years after that, William Cummings, a young English organist, picked up those words and that melody, and created one of the most perfect and best-loved carols of all! Teamwork won through in the end – and I can just imagine God smiling at the blessing it's given us all.

Pam Rhodes, broadcaster and author

Day 19

Beyond human understanding

Rejoice in the Lord always. I will say it again: rejoice! Let your gentleness be evident to all. The Lord is near. Do not be anxious about anything, but in every situation, by prayer and petition, with thanksgiving, present your requests to God. And the peace of God, which transcends all understanding, will guard your hearts and your minds in Christ Jesus.

Finally, brothers and sisters, whatever is true, whatever is noble, whatever is right, whatever is pure, whatever is lovely, whatever is admirable – if anything is excellent or praiseworthy – think about such things.

PHILIPPIANS 4:4–8

Reflection

I certainly don't think that Christians live totally peace-filled lives without anxiety. We are humans, with a natural bent towards worry when difficulties arise. I think that is why we are encouraged so much in the Bible not to be afraid, or allow our hearts to be troubled. When the automatic response is fear, how do we learn to let go of it and hold on to peace instead? I think what we learned in day 15 is a key to this, and it is mentioned again here: to be thankful to God in all circumstances.

It is so easy to allow our minds to fixate on our problems. My family and I have had some rather all-consuming difficulties recently, and there have been times when I have felt completely overwhelmed. I have needed to carefully research and then take action, but I have also noticed a huge difference in my own sense of well-being when I go first to God in prayer and offer the situations to him. I have also learned to recognise (with the help of my husband) when my mind is refusing to budge from focusing on the problem. This is something I find hard, but taking time to meditate on the truths about who God is, which I often do through *lectio divina* or through worship, floods my heart with a sense of peace.

It doesn't make sense when times are tough for us to be able to feel at peace, and yet we know that God's peace 'transcends all understanding'. We are living in a time in history where there is so much uncertainty, and it is so easy to be caught up in a general sense of unease.

And yet we are told to 'take captive every thought to make it obedient to Christ' (2 Corinthians 10:5). We are interconnected beings, and there is certainly a connection between what we think about, how we feel and how we behave. Too many of us fill our days with endless scrolling online, taking in lots of negative information that we don't need to. It is important to be proactive about ensuring that we protect our hearts and minds – and allow space for Jesus' peace to come.

Prayer

Lord Jesus, help me to understand the link between thanksgiving, prayer and receiving your peace. Help me to be more aware of what I fill my mind with.

A Christmas blessing

May the joy of the angels,
the eagerness of the shepherds,
the perseverance of the wise men,
the obedience of Joseph and Mary
and the peace of the Christ-child
be yours this Christmas.

Prayer of blessing (Christmas) from *Common Worship*

Christmas is a time filled with so many emotions, the good and the bad. This short blessing always speaks right to the heart of the kind of Christmas I hope for in my own home and in the homes of others. A Christmas season filled with joy, eagerness, perseverance, obedience and, most of all, peace.

Imogen Ball, writer and curate at All Saints, Trull,
and St Michael's, Angersleigh

Day 20

Being a peacemaker

Abigail acted quickly. She took two hundred loaves of bread, two skins of wine, five dressed sheep, five seahs of roasted grain, a hundred cakes of raisins and two hundred cakes of pressed figs, and loaded them on donkeys. Then she told her servants, 'Go on ahead; I'll follow you'…

When Abigail saw David, she… fell at his feet and said: 'Pardon your servant, my lord, and let me speak to you…'

David said to Abigail… 'May you be blessed for your good judgement and for keeping me from bloodshed this day… Go home in peace. I have heard your words and granted your request.'

1 SAMUEL 25:18–19, 23–24, 32–33, 35

Reflection

Not only does the Prince of Peace give us his peace, but we are also called to be his peacemakers. I love the Old Testament example of Abigail, and I encourage you to read her whole story in 1 Samuel 25 if you can. She was married to a foolish man, Nabal, who was tight-fisted and rude. He insulted David and his men, who were on the run from Saul, by refusing provision for them even though they had helped to protect his men and flock. The household's servant went direct to Abigail to tell her what had happened, recognising her wisdom. Thinking quickly, she went to meet David, and through her words and actions brought peace to what could have been a potentially life-threatening situation for her whole household.

We may never encounter such dire circumstances, but we will all experience times of tension in our workplaces, homes or places of study. Are we known as peace-makers in those places? Sometimes that may mean putting others' needs before our own, which we are encouraged to do (see Philippians 2:3–4). At other times it might necessitate being calm and gentle in our responses; as Proverbs 15:1 says: 'A gentle answer turns away wrath.' By simply being courteous and kind, we can share peace in each of the places we go to. But being a peacemaker is also about standing up for what is right. Abigail knew that David would have had blood on his hands if he had carried out his plans and, even though it put her own life in danger, she was willing to confront him to save the innocent lives within her household.

Are we willing to stand up for justice and help bring peace to our neighbours, both locally and around the globe? Being a peacemaker in such instances might mean we need to be active, perhaps by changing the brands that we buy, donating to and volunteering with local charities such as food banks, or praying for and writing to local and national government officials. There are so many ways we can actively demonstrate God's peace; why not ask him how he wants you to do that today?

Prayer

I am challenged by Abigail's example, Lord. She used the characteristics you provided her with to bring peace to a volatile situation, humbly and fearlessly. Teach me how you want me to share your peace with others too.

Christmas bells

I heard the bells on Christmas Day
their old familiar carols play,
and wild and sweet
the words repeat,
of 'Peace on earth, good will to men!'

And thought how, as the day had come,
the belfries of all Christendom
had rolled along
the unbroken song,
of 'Peace on earth, good will to men!'

Till ringing, singing on its way,
the world revolves from night to day,
a voice, a chime,
a chant sublime,
of 'Peace on earth, good will to men!'

And in despair I bowed my head,
'There is no peace on earth,' I said,
'For hate is strong
and mocks the song
of peace on earth, good will to men!'

Then pealed the bells more loud and deep,
'God is not dead, nor doth he sleep!
The wrong shall fail,
the right prevail,
with peace on earth, good will to men!'

Henry Wadsworth Longfellow (1807–82)

For the past 30 years, my father has put together an anthology of poetry every Christmas which gets sent out to all his friends and family instead of the ubiquitous Christmas card. It means I associate Christmas with poetry as much as with carols and turkey, and normally the poems in his booklets blend celebratory festive joy with a decent smattering of death and despair!

This poem by the US poet Henry Longfellow is one of his (and my) favourites. Amid the joyful bells and the refrain calling for 'peace on earth' is the stark reality that 'hate is strong and mocks the song'. But the final verse is hopeful: the bells are 'more loud and deep', and they proclaim that in the end 'the wrong shall fail' and there will indeed be 'peace on earth, good will to men!'

Clare Hayns, college chaplain, Christ Church, Oxford

Love

O holy night

O holy night, the stars are brightly shining,
it is the night of the dear Saviour's birth;
long lay the world in sin and error pining,
till he appeared and the soul felt its worth.
A thrill of hope – the weary world rejoices,
for yonder breaks a new and glorious morn;

Fall on your knees, Oh hear the angel voices!
O night divine, O night when Christ was born.
O night, O holy night, O night divine.

Words by Placide Cappeau (1808–77),
translated by John Sullivan Dwight (1813–93);
music by Adolphe Adam (1803–56)

A few years ago, I spent a lot of time listening to this song through Advent. It sings so gorgeously of the longing at the heart of Advent, and the gift at the heart of Christmas. I made, as gifts for friends, Christmas tree decorations inspired by its words. Each friend received a gift tag, with a line or two from the song painted on it and a little pearl bead tied to the top of the tag – as a kind of symbol of the treasure held within the words. It is an incredible gift to write to someone words like 'the soul felt its worth', 'a thrill of hope' and 'the weary world rejoices'. These are all astonishing reminders of what it means for God to draw near to us in Christ: at Christmas, we find that we are loved so much that God draws so close as to become one of us. Our weary world sings with joy, and our souls find their home.

Hannah Fytche, author and youth worker

'O holy night' is like the little black dress of Christmas carols! The melody is classy, chic, yet powerful in the message it sends. There is no need for vocal acrobatics with 'O holy night'; it simply requires being sung from the heart. And the line 'Fall on your knees' just says it all: a king is born and a weary world can rejoice and fall on its knees at the hope this news brings.

Esther Kuku, director of communications and Premier Gospel radio presenter

I particularly love the line 'Till he appeared and the soul felt its worth'. What a profound truth, expressed so simply. We have always had worth, loved as we were from before the creation of all things by the one who made us and who knows us absolutely. Yet that immense, unending love wrapped itself in a tiny infant body and began to live among us, that we might feel our worth. When the world tells us we don't count, one look at the face of Jesus tells us we matter; we have worth beyond all telling.

Lyndall Bywater, writer, speaker and broadcaster

'O holy night' is the one you will hear me singing most days in the run-up to Christmas. It's not just that this is a beautifully composed carol, but it speaks of social justice as part of God's great rescue mission:

> Truly he taught us to love one another;
> his law is love and his gospel is peace.
> Chains shall he break, for the slave is our brother,
> and in his name all oppression shall cease.

This is the God we serve, and for me, it should be sung all year round.

Charmaine Noble-McLean, director of content, Premier

Day 21

The reason he came

No one has ever gone into heaven except the one who came from heaven – the Son of Man. Just as Moses lifted up the snake in the wilderness, so the Son of Man must be lifted up, that everyone who believes may have eternal life in him.

For God so loved the world that he gave his one and only Son, that whoever believes in him shall not perish but have eternal life. For God did not send his Son into the world to condemn the world, but to save the world through him.

JOHN 3:13–17

Reflection

As I turned to write the final theme of these devotions, love, I simply had to start with John 3:16. It forms part of a conversation between Jesus and Nicodemus, who was trying to understand exactly who Jesus was. In response, Jesus affirmed the very reason that he walked the earth: love. It was because of love that the Father, Son and Spirit agreed that Jesus would come to earth as a baby. Just imagine what that conversation between them would have been like! The Trinity, full of love, agreeing to a course of action that would result in such suffering both for the Son and for the Father, seeing his Son's suffering but having agreed not to intervene. This was done because they knew it was the only way to save humankind.

We read throughout scripture of the way in which God drew near to his people. Providing a set of laws and sacrifices enabled some sort of communion with them, and yet over and over again they made mistakes or chose to run after other things. How that must have pained God's heart and yet, fuelled by love, he put into place a plan that would allow us direct access to him at all times – if we choose it.

When Jesus agreed to come to earth as a helpless baby, he knew where he was headed – to the cross. His remit was to provide salvation for all those who accepted him as their Lord. What an incredible truth! As I mentioned previously, too often we focus simply on his coming at Christmas and save our considerations of the cost of the cross for Easter, but let's take time to meditate on the whole story today.

This is the ultimate example of love in action. Love is not passive; rather, it is self-sacrificing. We will look more closely at the characteristics of love in the coming days, but today perhaps you could pray about who God wants you to share his love with, through the whole story of the gospel. We can be so quiet about our faith, and yet what a gift salvation would be for someone this Christmas! We can't make that happen, but we can respond to God's prompts to share our own experiences of his love.

Prayer

Lord, I thank you so much for your love, which cost you everything.

Love came down at Christmas

Love came down at Christmas,
love all lovely, love divine,
love was born at Christmas;
star and angels gave the sign.

Worship we the Godhead,
love incarnate, love divine;
worship we our Jesus,
but wherewith for sacred sign?

Love shall be our token;
love be yours and love be mine;
love to God and all men,
love for plea and gift and sign.

Christina Rossetti (1830–94)

When he was young, my son would add his Star Wars figures to our nativity scene at Christmas. Removing them each evening would get me thinking how we would explain the strange but wonderful Christmas story to alien lifeforms. An all-powerful and all-knowing God coming down to earth as a helpless baby in a manger – what's that really all about? In Christina Rossetti's poem, which I make sure I read each Christmas, we have a beautiful summary of the reason for the season. After all, the magnificent story of Christmas can be summed up in one little word – love.

Trystan Owain Hughes, MTh (theology) lead, St Padarn's Institute, Cardiff

Day 22

The faithfulness of God's love

When the Lord began to speak through Hosea, the Lord said to him, 'Go, marry a promiscuous woman and have children with her, for like an adulterous wife this land is guilty of unfaithfulness to the Lord'…

'Go, show your love to your wife again, though she is loved by another man and is an adulteress'…

It was I who taught Ephraim to walk, taking them by the arms… I led them with cords of human kindness, with ties of love…

'I will heal their waywardness and love them freely, for my anger has turned away from them.'

HOSEA 1:2; 3:1; 11:3–4; 14:4

Reflection

The book of Hosea beautifully reflects God's love for his people. He raised up the prophet Hosea and told him to marry a woman who would be unfaithful to him. Her actions would mirror those of Israel's and be a prophetic warning to the people.

Just think about the cost to Hosea of marrying Gomer, showing her love and having children with her, but watching her be drawn away from him and becoming adulterous. And then think about how this reflects the story of Israel's relationship to God – and our own.

In Hosea 3 the prophet, under God's instruction, sought out his wayward wife and even paid to take her back. In the same way, we know that God was willing to pay the price to redeem us.

Hosea 11 is a beautiful picture of how tender and compassionate God was towards Israel – like a doting father teaching his child to walk. He so longed for his chosen nation to learn how to live in relationship with him, but the Israelites kept turning away. Throughout the book we see their unfaithfulness and, like a father discipling his children, there is a cycle of God's judgement and then restoration offered; the latter Hosea acts out symbolically by offering the same to his unfaithful wife. This book reminds us that even when 'we are faithless, he remains faithful, for he cannot disown himself' (2 Timothy 2:13).

We can read this story and feel somewhat detached from it, but the sin God held against Israel was the fact they kept wandering away from him, looking to other things to satisfy, and only came back when they were uncomfortable. In an age that values instant gratification, we can, in fact, act similarly. Anything that takes a higher place in our hearts than God makes us unfaithful before him.

This book is one that I hold close to my heart, as it spoke to my husband in a crisis time in our marriage. The way he responded to me, much like Hosea, revealed the love of Jesus to me in a way I had never known before. I have learned, sometimes through painful mistakes, how God continually woos us. When we turn to him in repentance, his arms are open wide, expressing perfect love.

Prayer

Lord, I thank you that, even when I am unfaithful, you never are. I can count on your love – always.

Come, thou fount of every blessing

Come, thou fount of every blessing;
tune my heart to sing thy grace;
streams of mercy, never ceasing,
call for songs of loudest praise.
Teach me some melodious sonnet,
sung by flaming tongues above;
praise the mount! I'm fixed upon it,
mount of God's unchanging love!

O to grace how great a debtor
daily I'm constrained to be!
Let that grace now, like a fetter,
bind my wandering heart to thee.
Prone to wander, Lord, I feel it,
prone to leave the God I love;
here's my heart; O take and seal it;
seal it for thy courts above.

Words by Robert Robinson (1735–90);
composers include John Wyeth (1770–1858)

Even though I know, as a Christian, that Christmas is all about Jesus, it's still so easy during this bustling season to find myself distracted, drawn into gifts rather than *the* Gift, presents rather than his presence, shiny lights rather than the light of the world. I love praying this hymn all year round, including at Christmas, because it's a helpful reminder that, left to my own devices, I'm prone to wander, but my heart's desire is to find myself fixed on and bound to my beautiful Saviour Jesus.

Natalie Williams, chief executive, Jubilee+

Day 23

Jesus on love

A s the Father has loved me, so have I loved you. Now remain in my love. If you keep my commands, you will remain in my love, just as I have kept my Father's commands and remain in his love. I have told you this so that my joy may be in you and that your joy may be complete. My command is this: love each other as I have loved you. Greater love has no one than this: to lay down one's life for one's friends.

JOHN 15:9–13

Reflection

This passage shows us the way in which we are linked to God's bigger story: he first loved Jesus; he showed his love for us by sending Jesus (see day 21); Jesus loved us by agreeing to come as a baby to a hurting world; and here he was preparing his disciples for life after his death, resurrection and ascension. The text seems so simple and yet it is hugely profound: to remain in God's love requires obedience; there is a joy to be found for both us and Jesus when we remain in his love (how incredible); Jesus asks us to love others as he has loved us.

What a privilege, but also a huge responsibility. Jesus touches on how sacrificial loving one another can be, but in this passage concentrates on loving within friendships. He went even further in his sermon on the mount, calling for us to love our enemies as well as our friends:

> You have heard that it was said, 'Love your neighbour and hate your enemy.' But I tell you, love your enemies and pray for those who persecute you, that you may be children of your Father in heaven.
>
> MATTHEW 5:43–45

This season, let us take time to think about whether we are remaining in Jesus' love. Are we keeping his commandments? Are we following him closely and showing love to others in the way that he did? What does loving others well look like in our own personal contexts? How do we share Jesus' love to those in our neighbourhood? What about responding in loving ways when others do something that annoys us, such as cutting us up in traffic or speaking behind our backs?

In our 'me-centred', busy culture, it can be a challenge to lay down our lives for our friends. But this could be as simple as sending an encouraging message or phoning/ video calling a friend to see how they are. Do we make ourselves available to others when they need us to set aside our own plans in order to help them? It is worth pondering our heart attitude today.

Prayer

Lord, thank you that you taught us to remain in your love. Prompt me today to reach out in love to friends and family, and to respond lovingly to those who may wrong me.

Bethlehem Down

When he is King we will give him the King's gifts,
myrrh for its sweetness, and gold for a crown,
'beautiful robes', said the young girl to Joseph
fair with her first-born on Bethlehem Down.

Bethlehem Down is full of the starlight
winds for the spices, and stars for the gold,
Mary for sleep, and for lullaby music
songs of a shepherd by Bethlehem fold.

When he is King they will clothe him in grave-sheets,
myrrh for embalming, and wood for a crown,
he that lies now in the white arms of Mary
sleeping so lightly on Bethlehem Down.

Here he has peace and a short while for dreaming,
close-huddled oxen to keep him from cold,
Mary for love, and for lullaby music
songs of a shepherd by Bethlehem fold.

Words by Bruce Blunt (1899–1957);
music by Peter Warlock (1894–1930)

My favourite carol is 'Bethlehem Down', composed in 1927 by Peter Warlock (the pseudonym of Philip Arnold Heseltine), setting a poem written by journalist and poet Bruce Blunt. I love this carol because of its intense beauty and power. The words set a scene of peace and joy at the manger, but the third verse points to the suffering and death Christ will endure. I also love the carol because of the unusual way it came about. Warlock and Blunt were short of money and wanted to pay for an 'immortal carouse' (a heavy bout of drinking) over Christmas. On a walk between two pubs one night they composed the words and the tune. The carol was submitted to *The Daily Telegraph*'s Christmas carol contest, and it won.

The motivations for the carol's composition may not have been entirely honourable or praiseworthy, but the story illuminates the truth that grace, beauty and divinity can shine out from the most unlikely places. The transcendent can be found amid the gritty reality of our human existence, reminding us of the transforming power of the incarnation itself.

Jonathan Arnold, executive director of the Social Justice Network, Canterbury Diocese

Day 24

The greatest of all

Love is patient, love is kind. It does not envy, it does not boast, it is not proud. It does not dishonour others, it is not self-seeking, it is not easily angered, it keeps no record of wrongs. Love does not delight in evil but rejoices with the truth. It always protects, always trusts, always hopes, always perseveres.

Love never fails…

And now these three remain: faith, hope and love. But the greatest of these is love.

1 CORINTHIANS 13:4–8, 13

Reflection

This passage is often read out at weddings, but, for me, it is also a great summary of Christmas. It is at this time of year that we seek to show our love for others in the presents we carefully choose for them and the time we carve out for them. But of course, the greatest gift of Christmas is Jesus Christ himself.

This description of love is beautiful, but also demanding. It describes the love that we are offered by our Saviour, but it is also the love we are to show others. Rather than being selfish, it looks to serve others. Rather than storing up a record of all the wrongs someone has done to us, ready to throw back at them in a fight, it actively chooses not to. Rather than giving up or in easily, it fights on with hope and perseverance.

To home in on the start of this passage: I know that I can lack patience at times, but when I look at the life of Jesus I can see how patient he was – with his disciples when they seemed to lack understanding, with the crowds and even with his enemies. Jesus was also kind to those around him, stopping to touch those he recognised were looking to him with faith. In Romans 2:4 Paul explains, 'God's kindness is intended to lead you to repentance.' His kindness draws us closer to his love.

How easy it is to be envious of others – even at Christmas! Perhaps someone else receives the present you secretly wanted, or has family visiting when you are alone, or is able to buy expensive presents when you are struggling to make ends meet.

But, through Jesus, we can learn to be content in whatever circumstances we find ourselves (see Philippians 4:11–13); in fact, thanking Jesus for his coming and for all the love he has shown is a great antidote to envy.

So many of the attributes given to love in this passage seem countercultural today, and yet, as this chapter starts: 'If I speak in the tongues of men or of angels, but do not have love, I am only a resounding gong or a clanging cymbal' (1 Corinthians 13:1). This Christmas, let's look to reflect Jesus' love rather than our culture.

Prayer

Lord Jesus, I know I cannot be patient, kind or any of these other things in my own strength. Please help me to reflect your love to those around me.

Christmas Eve

Christmas hath a darkness
Brighter than the blazing noon,
Christmas hath a chillness
Warmer than the heat of June,
Christmas hath a beauty
Lovelier than the world can show:
For Christmas bringeth Jesus,
Brought for us so low.

Earth, strike up your music,
Birds that sing and bells that ring;
Heaven hath answering music
For all Angels soon to sing:
Earth, put on your whitest
Bridal robe of spotless snow:
For Christmas bringeth Jesus,
Brought for us so low.

Christina Rossetti (1830–94)

I have always loved Rossetti's carol 'In the bleak midwinter', but then discovered her other Christmas poems. 'Christmas Eve' is full of paradox. It seems simple on first reading, but takes us deeply into the themes of Advent running up to Christmas: darkness and light, winter and spring, heaven and earth coming together. Each phrase repays careful contemplation to yield its many layers, especially the last couplet: 'Christmas bringeth Jesus, Brought for us so low.' As we teeter on the brink of Christmas morning, we are led to wonder once more at God's amazing gift.

Liz Hoare, tutor in spiritual formation, Wycliffe Hall, Oxford

Day 25

Always connected

C hrist Jesus who died – more than that, who was raised to life – is at the right hand of God and is also interceding for us. Who shall separate us from the love of Christ? Shall trouble or hardship or persecution or famine or nakedness or danger or sword?… I am convinced that neither death nor life, neither angels nor demons, neither the present nor the future, nor any powers, neither height nor depth, nor anything else in all creation, will be able to separate us from the love of God that is in Christ Jesus our Lord.

ROMANS 8:34–35, 38–39

Reflection

As we draw to the end of our reflections, I want to point us to the incredible, eternal truth that we are always connected to God's love through Jesus. We have seen how Jesus is God's greatest gift to us – not only because he came to earth and died for our sins, but also because he was resurrected, ascended and is now seated next to God, interceding on our behalf every day. How incredible is that? Take a moment to picture Jesus in the following ways: as a baby lying in his manger; speaking words of comfort to his mother as he hung on the cross; seated next to his heavenly Father speaking words of intercession for you into his Father's ear.

Christmas is meant to be a time of joy, a season of celebration and fun. And yet it doesn't take away the hardships that many of us are facing in the form of long-term physical or mental illnesses, family estrangements, bereavements, poverty. I am also struck by the word 'persecution' in today's passage; while we might not be facing immediate, life-threatening persecution ourselves, so many around the world are. Just today I read what Jesus had to say about such persecution to his disciples: 'Do not be afraid of those who kill the body but cannot kill the soul' (Matthew 10:28). He went on to reiterate God's care, and that is what is so amazing about the truth in our Romans passage: whatever we face in this life, absolutely nothing can separate us from his love. What an incredible promise to celebrate this Christmas!

The phrase 'neither height nor depth' reminds me of what Paul said to the Ephesians, and I echo it for you:

> I pray that you, being rooted and established in love, may have power, together with all the Lord's holy people, to grasp how wide and long and high and deep is the love of Christ, and to know this love that surpasses knowledge – that you may be filled to the measure of all the fullness of God.

EPHESIANS 3:17–19

It is as his love permeates our very beings that we can rest secure in it. May the love, peace, joy, faith and hope to be found in Jesus fill you this Christmas time.

Prayer

Jesus, I thank you that absolutely nothing can separate me from your love.
Open my eyes to see your love at work in my life today.

What child is this?

What child is this, who, laid to rest
On Mary's lap is sleeping?
Whom angels greet with anthems
sweet,
While shepherds watch are keeping?
This, this is Christ the King,
Whom shepherds worship and
angels sing:
Haste, haste to bring him praise
The Babe, the son of Mary.

Why lies he in such mean estate,
Where ox and ass are feeding?
Come, have no fear, God's son is here,
His love all loves exceeding:
Nails, spear, shall pierce him
through,
The cross be borne for me, for you:
Hail, hail, the Saviour comes,
The Babe, the son of Mary.

So bring him incense, gold
and myrrh,
All tongues and peoples own him,
The King of kings salvation brings,
Let every heart enthrone him:
Raise, raise your song on high
While Mary sings a lullaby,
Joy, joy, for Christ is born,
The Babe, the son of Mary.

William Chatterton Dix (1837–98)

154

To me, this is *the* Christmas carol, because it combines the sacred and secular in a blend of music and words that reminds us that Christmas is both nowadays. Using the traditional English melody 'Greensleeves', with its resonances of unrequited love and concluding plea, 'Come once again and love me', Dix asks us questions about a greater, also perhaps unrequited, love, which comes again each year in the babe of Bethlehem to dwell among us as light and Saviour of the world. Like the original folk song, this hymn has a bittersweet flavour, for in verse two we hear of the 'mean estate': the poor location of the manger, where, as sinners, we are entreated to be fearful. Be afraid, Dix warns us; be very afraid, for this silent, sleeping child, though he be the son of Mary, is the Word made flesh. The ever-so-human description of verse one is giving way to the theological meaning of this baby, of whom we may well ask: 'What child is this?'

At Christmas, let us peer deeper and try to explore the significance of the Word made flesh, of Christ our King, and the way in which the human baby son of Mary can be both of these. In this carol we can never avoid the sense that there is more than humanity being described. And if we can grasp the dual nature of this human–divine child – asleep in Mary's arms, but also awake to the sin of the world – then we, too, will wish to make haste to 'bring him laud' and raise his song on high!

Gordon Giles, canon chancellor, Rochester Cathedral

Index of quotations

Index of Bible passages

Meet our Christmas Voices...

Naomi Aidoo is a coach and founder of Time & Pace®, helping people with big goals and little time. She is also director of digital and wellbeing for education company Innerscope. **Andy Angel** is director of formation for ministry in the Diocese of Oxford. He was formerly vicar of St Andrew's, Burgess Hill, and vice-principal of St John's College, Nottingham. **Jonathan Arnold** is executive director of the Social Justice Network in the Diocese of Canterbury. Before ordination he was a member of St Paul's Cathedral Choir and The Sixteen. **Imogen Ball** is a curate at All Saints, Trull, and St Michael's, Angersleigh. **Ruth M. Bancewicz** is church engagement director at The Faraday Institute for Science and Religion, Cambridge. **Carl Beech** leads Edge Ministries and the Edge Faith Community. He is also the president of Christian Vision for Men. **John L. Bell** is a hymn writer and Church of Scotland minister. He is a member of the Iona Community, a broadcaster and a former student activist. **Andrew Boakye** is a New Testament critic, lecturing in religions and theology at the University of Manchester. **Catherine Butcher** is a professional editor and journalist. She has edited a number of magazines, including *Woman Alive* and *Renewal*. **Lyndall Bywater** is a freelance speaker and writer. Previously The Salvation Army's UK prayer coordinator, she is now part of Connecting the Isles and 24-7 Prayer's Europe team. Author, spiritual director and retreat leader, **Mags Duggan** has worked with the Navigators as a cross-cultural missionary in East Asia, Hong Kong and Taiwan. **Hannah Fytche** is a PhD student in New Testament theology at the University of Cambridge, an author and a blogger. **Gordon Giles** is canon chancellor of Rochester Cathedral, an editor of *Ancient and Modern* (2013) and a director of the English Hymnal Company. **Paul W. Goodliff** is a Baptist minister, pastoral theologian, lecturer, trainer, poet, author and former general secretary of Churches Together in England. **Isabelle Hamley** is theological adviser to the House of Bishops (Church of England). She was previously chaplain to the Archbishop of Canterbury, vicar, theological college lecturer and university chaplain. **Clare Hayns** is college chaplain at Christ Church, Oxford. Before ordination she was a social worker and also ran an events company. **Liz Hoare** is an ordained Anglican priest and teaches spiritual formation at Wycliffe Hall, Oxford. **Trystan Owain Hughes** is tutor in applied theology at St Padarn's Institute and priest-in-charge of Christ Church, Roath Park, Cardiff. He has also contributed regularly to BBC Radio 2 and BBC Radio 4. **Lakshmi Jeffreys** is rector of a parish just outside Northampton. **Andy Kind** is a promedian (preacher and comedian) and writer. **David Kitchen** is a poet, broadcaster, teacher and storyteller who has been making the Bible come alive for longer than he cares to remember. **Esther Kuku** is director of communications and engagement at the Resuscitation Council UK and a radio presenter for Premier Gospel. **Martin Leckebusch** is one of the UK's most prolific contemporary hymn writers. **Bekah Legg** is CEO of Restored, a Christian organisation with a mission to speak up about violence against women and equip the church to stand against domestic abuse and support survivors. **Ann Lewin** is a poet, author and speaker who taught RE and English for 27 years before working as a welfare adviser to international university students. **Tanya Marlow** is an author, speaker and broadcaster on faith and spirituality. She also campaigns for those with chronic illness, disability and myalgic encephalomyelitis. **Leoné Martin** is an associate pastor at Cannon Street Memorial Baptist Church. **Chine McDonald** is director of the religion and society think tank Theos. She is a regular contributor to BBC Religion and Ethics programmes. **Lucy Moore** is the founder of Messy Church and head of the Church of England's Growing Faith Foundation. **Michele D. Morrison** is a freelance writer, wife, mother and grandmother and blogs at **tearsamidthealiencorn.blogspot.com**. **Charmaine Noble-McLean** is content director for Premier, having presented a variety of radio programmes and worked in television as an arts/entertainment correspondent. **Emma Pennington** is canon missioner for Canterbury Cathedral. Formerly a vicar in the Diocese of Oxford and chaplain of Worcester College, Oxford, she speaks widely about the spirituality of Julian of Norwich. **Pam Rhodes** is the familiar face of BBC Television's *Songs of Praise*, presenting programmes from tiny country churches to huge outside broadcasts, with interviews ranging from Pope John Paul II to Dolly Parton. **Amy Scott Robinson** is an author, poet and performance storyteller. She is a regular contributor to the *Church Times* and provides online resources for Engage Worship. **Margaret Silf** is an ecumenical Christian committed to working across and beyond traditional divisions. She is a retreat facilitator and author of a number of books for 21st-century spiritual pilgrims. **Meric Srokosz** is professor of physical oceanography at the National Oceanography Centre, Southampton. He is a former associate director of the Faraday Institute for Science and Religion. **Jo Swinney** has eight books to her name and has written frequently for Christian publications across the UK and beyond. She is director of communications for A Rocha International. **Rachele Evelyn (Evie) Vernon O'Brien** is a nannyish (Jamaican womanist liberation) theologian and Anglican deacon, based at St Mildred's Church in Croydon. **Sally Welch** is diocesan canon of Christ Church Cathedral, Oxford and co-director of the Centre for Christian Pilgrimage. **Natalie Williams** is chief executive of Jubilee+, which equips UK churches to change the lives of those in poverty in their communities.